Blackstone's
ANNUAL UPDATE
1991

PERSONAL INJURY

Blackstone's
ANNUAL UPDATE
1991

PERSONAL INJURY

Derek Morgan BA
Senior Fellow in Health Care Law,
University College Swansea

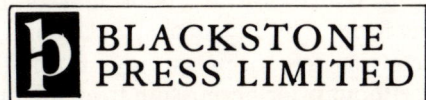

First published in Great Britain 1991 by Blackstone Press Limited,
9-15 Aldine Street, London W12 8AW.
Telephone 081-740 1173

© D. Morgan, 1991

ISBN: 1 85431 133 6

British Library Cataloguing in Publication Data
A CIP catalogue record for this book is available from the British Library

Typeset by Murdoch Evans Partnership, Tonbridge
Printed by BPCC Wheatons Ltd, Exeter

All rights reserved. No part of this book may be reproduced or transmitted in any form or by any means, electronic or mechanical, including photocopying, recording, or any information storage or retrieval system without prior permission from the publisher.

CONTENTS

	Preface	ix
1	**Statutes**	1
	Social Security Act 1989, s. 22 and sch. 4	1
	Social Security Act 1990, s. 7 and sch. 1	1
	Courts and Legal Services Act 1990	25
2	**Statutory Instruments**	27
	Social Security (Recoupment) Regulations 1990	27
	Rules of the Supreme Court (Amendment No. 2) 1990	35
	Rules of the Supreme Court (Amendment No. 4) 1989	37
	County Court (Amendment No. 4) Rules 1989	37
	Civil Legal Aid (Assessment of Resources) Regulations 1989	39
	Civil Legal Aid (Assessment of Resources) (Amendment) Regulations 1990	39
	Rules of the Supreme Court (Amendment) 1990	41
	County Court (Amendment) Rules 1990	41
	Road Traffic Accidents (Payment for Treatment) Order 1990	42
3	**Cases**	43
	Liability	43
	Jones v Chief Constable of South Yorkshire	43
	Rance v Mid Downs Health Authority	46

CONTENTS

B v Islington Health Authority 48
F v Wirral Metropolitan Borough Council 50
Jones v Northampton Borough Council 51
Kirkham v Chief Constable of the Greater
 Manchester Police 52
Pitts v Hunt 53
Morris v Murray 54
Smith v Ainger 55
Eastman v South West Thames Health
 Authority 57
Porter v Barking and Dagenham LBC 58
White v St Albans City and District Council 58
Whitfield v H & R Johnson (Tiles) Ltd 60
De Souza v Home and Overseas Insurance Co Ltd ... 60
Hughes v Waltham Forest Health Authority 61

Damages 62
Pidduck v Eastern Scottish Omnibuses 62
Wood v British Coal Corporation 63
Corbett v Barking, Havering and Brentwood Health
 Authority 64
Stanley v Saddique 66
Champion v London Fire and Civil Defence
 Authority 68
Middleton v Elliott Turbo Machinery 69
Quantum of Damages: Personal Injuries or Death ... 71

Practice and Procedure 77
Re HIV Haemophiliac Litigation 77
Singh v London Underground 78
Donovan v Gwentoys Ltd 79
Guidera v NEI Projects (India) Ltd 81
Stephen v Riverside Health Authority 81
Halford v Brookes 82
Bentley v Bristol and Western Health Authority 84
Jones v Trollope and Colls Cementation
 Overseas Ltd 85
Foster v Turnbull 86
Kelly v Dawes 87
Chrzanowska v Glaxo Laboratories 89

CONTENTS

	Horrocks v Ford Motor Co Ltd	90
	O'Connor v Amos Bridgman Abattoirs Ltd	91
	Lindop v Goodwin Steel Castings Ltd	92
	Wilson v Graham	92
	Thomas v Bunn, Wilson v Graham and Lea v British Aerospace	93
	Gee v News Group Newspaper Ltd	96
	Legal Aid Board v Russell	97
	Doleman v Deakin	99
	Schott Kem Ltd v Bentley	100
4	**Official Publications**	103
	Master of the Rolls' Review of the Legal Year 1989-90	103
	Practice Note: Transfer of damages awarded in the Queen's Bench Division to the Court of Protection	104
	Practice Direction: Supreme Court Taxing Office	105
	Practice Direction: Queen's Bench Division	106
	Crown Indemnity Scheme: Department of Health Circular (HC(89)34)	106
	EC Council Directive 90/269/EEC	107
	EC Council Directive 90/270/EEC	108
	Provision of Service to the Inner London Residuary Body: Personal Injury Claims (ILEA)	109
5	**Commercial Publications and other Important Sources**	111
	Butterworths Personal Injury Litigation Service by Iain Goldrein and Margaret de Haas	111
	Kemp and Kemp: The Quantum of Damages by David A. Mcl. Kemp	111
	Articles on Structured Settlements	112

PREFACE

Last year was an exceptionally busy year for the personal injuries lawyer, and the formation of the Association of Personal Injuries Lawyers as a mutual support group attests to the fact.

In selecting items for inclusion in this review, obvious candidates have included the detailed recoupment regulations for the offset of social security payments against awards of damages; the introduction of reforms bringing automatic directions and provisional damages to the county court; the 'nervous shock' or 'Post Traumatic Stress Disorder' developments following the Hillsborough Stadium disaster in Sheffield; the unabated flow of litigation generated by the Limitation Act 1980; and, more generally, judicial developments in awards of damages and the use of structured settlements, interim payments and the fashioning of guidance for the conduct of multi-plaintiff actions (the so called 'mass tort' claims). Otherwise, I have tried in this short compass to select what seem to me to be either the highlights of the year or useful illustrations of where personal injuries litigation practice might be developed or explored. What follows then is not intended to be a comprehensive catalogue, but more of a sampler.

I am particularly grateful to my editor at Blackstone Press, Mandy Preece, for her patience, fortitude and perseverance with a manuscript which on more than one occasion she despaired of ever seeing. There were times in December 1990 when I knew how she must have felt.

Derek Morgan
Abergavenny, Gwent

1

STATUTES

Social Security Act 1989, s. 22 and sch. 4
Social Security Act 1990, s. 7 and sch. 1

Social security recoupment

Under s. 2 of the Law Reform (Personal Injuries) Act 1948 a defendant in a personal injuries action was entitled to deduct from the damages in respect of loss of earnings payable to a successful plaintiff 50 per cent of certain specific benefits and the full value of some others. The amount which the defendant so deducted was, in effect, a 'windfall' benefit as far as the defendant was concerned, because that amount was not repayable to the state. That has now changed with the radical revisions introduced by the Social Security Act 1989, s. 22 and sch. 4 and the Recoupment Regulations 1990, which came into effect on 3 September 1990 (see Chapter 2). Amendments to the 1989 Act were secured before it came into effect by the Social Security Act 1990, s. 7 and sch. 1.

The 1948 Act provisions are drastically modified, and will apply now only to exempt 'small payments' which are discussed below. The measure first recommended by Beveridge and endorsed by the Pearson Commission in 1978 is now introduced; statutory benefits are fully deducted. And the deduction is against the entire payment of damages, that is including general damages for pain, suffering and shock, and not just against the special damages for loss of earnings, as was the case under the 1948 legislation. This has massive implications for all who are involved in personal injury litigation. It may also introduce a new source of delay in settling claims.

The 'clawback' scheme

The Act introduces a new scheme which allows the Department of Social Security to reclaim from a defendant social security benefits paid to a plaintiff who has suffered an accident or an industrial disease, whether the 'compensation payment' is made by way of an award under a court order or an out of court settlement, and whether or not liability has been admitted (1989 Act, s. 22(3)). Any such repayments under the scheme are not reduced by a finding of contributory negligence. The new statutory scheme — or 'clawback' as it has become widely known — applies to all claims where:

(a) the plaintiff has received payment of one of the 'relevant' benefits enumerated in the Recoupment Regulations (see Chapter 2);

(b) the settlement of the claim is for £2,500 or more;

(c) the injury occurred (or the plaintiff received benefit for a named disease) on or after 1 January 1989.

Exempt payments

The most important of the 'exempt' compensation payments under s. 22(4) are:

(a) payments under the Fatal Accidents Act 1976;

(b) payments under the Vaccine Damage Payment Act 1979;

(c) awards made by the Criminal Injuries Compensation Board;

(d) any redundancy payment taken into account in the assessment of damages in respect of an injury, accident or disease;

(e) periodic payments made under the terms of a structured settlement for which special rules are provided;

(f) certain other payments, which are prescribed in the regulations (see Chapter 2);

(g) 'small' payments, those under the prescribed £2,500 limit (Social Security (Recoupment) Regulations 1990, SI 1990 No. 332, reg. 3), which is set rather higher than many personal injuries lawyers had originally expected. Sums under this amount will continue to be subject to the provisions of s. 2 of the 1948 Act (sch. 4, para. 22(2) of the 1989 Act, inserting new s. 2(1A) to the 1948 Act), but only where the 'relevant' social security benefits have in fact been paid to the injured party. Otherwise, they are excluded from the scheme (s. 22(6)). This sum of £2,500 originally included not only the compensation, but also the costs incurred in obtaining it. Thus if an award of £2,300 had associated costs of £200, it would have been subject to the clawback provision. A Law Society amendment to the Social Security Bill, now s. 7 and sch. 1, para. 1(1)(b) of the Social Security Act 1990, ensures that the clawback will apply only to the damages awarded and not the costs. Schedule 4, para. 4 is so worded as to prevent evasion of this scheme by dividing the payment into exempt 'bundles'.

Property damage; the MIB; interest on damages and payments into court
It is not clear, but it is widely thought that the statutory scheme does not include payments by way of compensation for property damage arising from an accident (see the intervention of Lord Henley in debate on the Social Security Bill 1990, Official Report, House of Lords, 11 July 1990). Section 7 and sch. 1, para. 1(1) of the 1990 Act makes it clear that the provisions as to clawback affect payments made by the Motor Insurers Bureau. Two final reforms made by the 1990 Act deal with interest on damages and payments into court (see below). Section 7 and sch. 1, para. 6 provide that when assessing the amount of interest payable, the amount of the award is treated as reduced by the amount to be recouped by the DSS; in other words, the plaintiff will not be entitled to interest on so much of his or her damages as is to be clawed back by the DSS. Any such reduction is to be applied first to special damages and then in respect of any balance, against the general damages.

There are a number of complex features of this new scheme which need attention; the detailed working out of its administration, which is conducted by the Compensation Recovery Unit of the DSS, will disclose practical matters which will be reviewed in later editions of this text.

Implications
As far as plaintiffs are concerned, double recovery of benefits and damages will no longer be available. The implications for defendants, their insurers and their advisers are more complicated; it implements the Government's view that the state should not provide a subsidy to tortfeasors. Effectively, the responsibility to make the recovery of the benefits paid is placed upon the defendant,

on behalf of the DSS. Upon receipt of a damages claim, the defendant must within 14 days notify the CRU on Form CRU1 (or an agreed computer generated form) of that fact. It is thought important to inform the CRU even of exempt payments as this will enable the compensator to seek details of the benefits when the claim reaches settlement stage. This will be necessary because even for small claims, the 50 per cent deduction under the 1948 Act remains active.

Before a settlement can be reached, the defendant must obtain from the DSS a certificate — CRU4 — of the total amount of benefit paid, which must be deducted from any award or settlement, and then repaid direct to the DSS. The CRU4 certificate, which will be issued to the compensator within four weeks of the notification of the claim to CRU, will remain valid for a further eight weeks and will show upon it the week by week amounts of benefit to be paid within that period. If the claim is settled within the eight week period, the compensator must deduct from the compensation the amount shown on the certificate and pay that to CRU within 14 days. When rendering this payment the compensator must inform CRU if it represents the final settlement of the claim. If the compensator fails to deduct the benefit but instead mistakenly pays it to the claimant, he or she remains liable to pay CRU, and DSS may take action to recover the benefit, as it may do so against a compensator who makes the relevant deductions but fails to make the payment of them to CRU. The scheme does not, however, give the DSS a right of subrogation, as properly understood.

The most immediate impact is that the loss of earnings element of any claim will increase as a burden on the defendant. Under the scheme, a defendant is no longer entitled to deduct from any loss of earnings claim either half of some benefits or 100 per cent of others. An amount equal to all the applicable specified benefits received will be included in the claim for loss of earnings and is deducted from the settlement. That sum is then repaid by the defendant to the DSS direct. The recoupment period for deduction is the 'relevant period' (the period up until the compensation payment is made) or for a period of five years from the date of the injury, whichever is the earlier (s. 23(3)). In most cases, of course, the compensation payment will be made within the five year period. Where costs are dealt with after quantum, the relevant period ends when the plaintiff receives a final payment.

STATUTES

Provisional damages and payments into court
Any provisional damages payment made within the five year period is disregarded for the purposes of a settlement for the purposes of the five year rule, except where the question of an appeal is raised. From sch. 4, para. 12 it is clear that the recoupment provisions do not make provision for deductions to be made in respect of monies paid into court. When making a payment in, the defendant must hold back the amount to be repaid to the DSS. Upon acceptance of the payment in, the defendant becomes liable to repay to the DSS an amount equal to the benefits received by the plaintiff. The defendant can obtain a certificate stating the amount of benefit to be repaid before he or she makes the payment in. That amount may then be withheld from the payment in. The defendant must inform the court of the amount withheld and provide the plaintiff with a statement of the total of the amount paid in and the amount of the benefits to be repaid. As far as payments into court are concerned, para. 12(2)(b) of sch. 4 to the 1989 Act is amended by the 1990 Act s. 7 and sch. 1, para. 2(2) so as to trigger liability to pay to the DSS upon notification to the compensator that not just the whole but part only of the monies paid into court have been paid out. Paragraph 12(5) originally provided that on payment out within 21 days, the relevant period (which means the period during which benefits may reduce compensation) would be deemed to have ended on the day of payment in. The amendments in sch. 1 to the 1990 Act provide that on acceptance within 21 days the relevant period is to be taken to have ended on the day of payment in or, if there were two or more payments in, on the day of the payment in of the last of the payments. The 'relevant period' ends on the day on which the compensator is notified of the payment out. In determining the amounts to which the DSS is entitled, the compensator is to be treated as if his or her payment in had been made on that day.

The court may of its own volition reduce the payment out by a sum equal to that of any relevant benefits paid to the plaintiff since the payment in (RSC ord. 22, r. 5(2) as amended by Rules of the Supreme Court (Amendment No. 2) 1990 (SI 1990 No. 1689), r. 18 and CRC ord. 11, r. 5(4) as amended by SI 1990 No. 1764, r. 22).

Those critics who argued that the 1948 compromise afforded a plaintiff a form of 'double recovery' have now been handsomely vindicated. There are some major difficulties which the administration of the scheme will yet disclose, but one important one which may be addressed here is whether the fact of full deduction deprives the claimant of all credit for national insurance contributions from which it may be argued he or she has earned the benefits; notice that not all the relevant benefits are payable by the DSS, particularly statutory sick pay. It will be interesting to see whether the practice develops of pleading the loss of national insurance contributions as part of the plaintiff's general damages claim.

One small illustration of the complexities in the workings of the recoupment scheme is illustrated in (1990) *New Law Journal* 1596 (15 November 1990). A solicitor involved in the Benzodiazepine litigation, which is now all dealt with by Legal Aid Area 7, had the original client's certificate issued out of Area 4, advancing £2,733 on account. When the certificate was discharged by Area 4 to be reissued in extended form by Area 7, the £2,733 was recouped from the firm's legal aid cheque. A reimbursement was promised four months later only following the firm's threat to sue to recover the wrongly deducted monies.

Social Security Act 1989 (as amended)

22. Recovery of sums equivalent to benefit from compensation payments in respect of accidents, injuries and diseases.

(1) A person (the 'compensator') making a compensation payment, whether on behalf of himself or another, in consequence of an accident, injury or disease suffered by any other person (the 'victim') shall not do so until the Secretary of State has furnished him with a certificate of total benefit and shall then—

(a) deduct from the payment an amount, determined in accordance with the certificate of total benefit, equal to the gross amount of any relevant benefits paid or likely to be paid to or for the victim during the relevant period in respect of that accident, injury or disease;

(b) pay to the Secretary of State an amount equal to that which is required to be so deducted;

(c) furnish the person to whom the compensation payment is or, apart from this section, would have been made (the 'intended recipient') with a certificate of deduction.

(2) Any right of the intended recipient to receive the compensation payment in question shall be regarded as satisfied to the extent of the amount certified in the certificate of deduction.

(3) In this section—
'benefit' means any benefit under—

(a) the Social Security Acts 1975 to 1988, or
(b) the Old Cases Act,
and the 'relevant benefits' are such of those benefits as may be prescribed for the purposes of this section;
'certificate of total benefit' means a certificate given by the Secretary of State in accordance with Schedule 4 to this Act;
'certificate of deduction' means a certificate given by the compensator specifying the amount which he has deducted and paid to the Secretary of State in pursuance of subsection (1) above;
'compensation payment' means any payment falling to be made (whether voluntarily, or in pursuance of a court order or an agreement, or otherwise)—
    (a) to or in respect of the victim in consequence of the accident, injury or disease in question, and
    (b) either (i) by or on behalf of a person who is, or is alleged to be, liable to any extent in respect of that accident, injury or disease, or (ii) in pursuance of a compensation scheme for motor accidents
but does not include benefit or an exempt payment or so much of any payment as is referable to costs incurred by any person;
'compensation scheme for motor accidents' means any scheme or arrangement under which funds are available for the payment of compensation in respect of motor accidents caused, or alleged to have been caused, by uninsured or unidentified persons;
'compensator', 'victim' and 'intended recipient' shall be construed in accordance with subsection (1) above;
'costs', in relation to proceedings in Scotland, means expenses;
'payment' means payment in money or money's worth, and cognate expressions shall be construed accordingly;
'relevant period' means—
    (a) in the case of a disease, the period of 5 years beginning with the date on which the victim first claims a relevant benefit in consequence of the disease; or
    (b) in any other case, the period of 5 years immediately following the day on which the accident or injury in question occurred;
but where before the end of that period the compensator makes a compensation payment in final discharge of any claim made by or in respect of the victim and arising out of the accident, injury or disease, the relevant period shall end on the date on which that payment is made.

(4) For the purposes of this section the following are the 'exempt payments'—
    (a) any small payment, as defined in paragraph 4 of Schedule 4 to this Act;
    (b) any payment made to or for the victim under section 35 of the Powers of Criminal Courts Act 1973 or section 58 of the Criminal Justice (Scotland) Act 1980;
    (c) any payment to the extent that it is made—
        (i) in consequence of an action under the Fatal Accidents Act 1976; or

(ii) in circumstances where, had an action been brought, it would have been brought under that Act;

(d) any payment to the extent that it is made in respect of a liability arising by virtue of section 1 of the Damages (Scotland) Act 1976;

(e) without prejudice to section 6(4) of the Vaccine Damage Payments Act 1979 (which provides for the deduction of any such payment in the assessment of any award of damages), any payment made under that Act to or in respect of the victim;

(f) any award of compensation made to or in respect of the victim by the Criminal Injuries Compensation Board under section 111 of the Criminal Justice Act 1988;

(g) any payment made in the exercise of a discretion out of property held subject to a trust in a case where no more than 50 per cent. by value of the capital contributed to the trust was directly or indirectly provided by persons who are, or are alleged to be, liable in respect of—

(i) the accident, injury or disease suffered by the victim in question; or

(ii) the same or any connected accident, injury or disease suffered by another;

(h) any payment made out of property held for the purposes of any prescribed trust (whether the payment also falls within paragraph (g) above or not);

(j) any payment made to the victim by an insurance company within the meaning of the Insurance Companies Act 1982 under the terms of any contract of insurance entered into between the victim and the company before—

(i) the date on which the victim first claims a relevant benefit in consequence of the disease in question; or

(ii) the occurrence of the accident or injury in question;

(k) any redundancy payment falling to be taken into account in the assessment of damages in respect of an accident, injury or disease.

(5) The Secretary of State may by regulations provide that any prescribed payment shall be an exempt payment for the purposes of this section.

(6) Except as provided by any other enactment, in the assessment of damages in respect of an accident, injury or disease the amount of any relevant benefits paid or likely to be paid shall be disregarded.

(7) Schedule 4 to this Act shall have effect for the purpose of supplementing the provisions of this section; and this section shall have effect subject to the provisions of that Schedule.

(8) This section and that Schedule shall apply in relation to any compensation payment made after the coming into force of this section to the extent that it is made in respect of—

(a) an accident or injury occurring on or after 1st January 1989; or

(b) a disease, if the victim's first claim for a relevant benefit in consequence of the disease is made on or after that date.

SCHEDULE 4

PART I

1. (1) In this Schedule—
'the recoupment provisions' means the provisions of section 22 of this Act and this Schedule;
'the relevant deduction' means the deduction required to be made from the compensation payment in question by virtue of the recoupment provisions;
'the relevant payment' means the payment required to be made to the Secretary of State by virtue of the recoupment provisions;
'the total benefit' means the gross amount referred to in section 22(1)(a) of this Act.
(2) If, after making the relevant deduction from the compensation payment, there would be no balance remaining for payment to the intended recipient, any reference in this Schedule to the making of the compensation payment shall be construed in accordance with regulations.
(3) Expressions used in this Schedule and in section 22 of this Act have the same meaning in this Schedule as they have in that section.

PART II

Time for making payment to Secretary of State

2. The compensator's liability to make the relevant payment arises immediately before the making of the compensation payment, and he shall make the relevant payment before the end of the period of 14 days following the day on which the liability arises.

The certificate of total benefit

3. (1) It shall be for the compensator to apply to the Secretary of State for the certificate of total benefit and he may, subject to sub-paragraph (5) below, from time to time apply for fresh certificates.
(2) The certificate of total benefit shall specify—
   (a) the amount which has been, or is likely to be, paid on or before a specified date by way of any relevant benefit which is capable of forming part of the total benefit;
   (b) where applicable—
      (i) the rate of any relevant benefit which is, has been, or is likely to be paid after the date so specified and which would be capable of forming part of the total benefit; and
      (ii) the intervals at which any such benefit is paid and the period for which it is likely to be paid;
   (c) the amounts (if any) which, by virtue of the recoupment provisions, are to be treated as increasing the total benefit; and
   (d) the aggregate amount of any relevant payments made on or before a specified date (reduced by so much of that amount as has been paid by the Secretary of State to the intended recipient before that date in consequence of the recoupment provisions).

(3) On issuing a certificate of total benefit, the Secretary of State shall be taken to have certified the total benefit as at every date for which it is possible to calculate an amount that would, on the basis of the information so provided, be the total benefit as at that date, on the assumption that payments of benefit are made on the days on which they first become payable.

(4) The Secretary of State may estimate, in such manner as he thinks fit, any of the amounts, rates or periods specified in the certificate of total benefit.

(5) A certificate of total benefit shall remain in force until such date as may be specified in the certificate for that purpose and no application for a fresh certificate shall be made before that date.

(6) Where a certificate ceases to be in force, the Secretary of State may issue a fresh certificate, whether or not an application has been made to him for such a certificate.

(7) The compensator shall not make the compensation payment at any time when there is no certificate of total benefit in force in respect of the victim, unless his liability to make the relevant deduction and the relevant payment has ceased to be enforceable by virtue of paragraph 15 below.

Exemption from deduction in cases involving small payments

4. (1) Regulations may make provision exempting persons from liability to make the relevant deduction or the relevant payment in prescribed cases where the amount of the compensation payment in question, or the aggregate amount of two or more connected compensation payments, does not exceed the prescribed sum.

(2) Regulations may make provision for cases where an amount has been deducted and paid to the Secretary of State which, by virtue of regulations under sub-paragraph (1) above, ought not to have been so deducted and paid, and any such regulations may, in particular, provide for him to pay that amount to the intended recipient or the compensator or to pay a prescribed part of it to each of them.

(3) The reference in section 22(4)(a) of this Act to a 'small payment' is a reference to a payment from which by virtue of this paragraph no relevant deduction falls to be made.

(4) For the purposes of this paragraph—
   (a) two or more compensation payments are 'connected' if each is made to or in respect of the same victim and in respect of the same accident, injury or disease; and
   (b) any reference to a compensation payment is a reference to a payment which would be such a payment apart from section 22(4)(a) of this Act.

Multiple compensation payments

5. (1) This paragraph applies where—
   (a) a compensation payment has been made (an 'earlier payment') to or in respect of the victim; and

(b) subsequently another such payment (a 'later payment') falls to be made to or in respect of the same victim in respect of the same accident, injury or disease (whether by the same or another compensator).

(2) In determining the amount of the relevant deduction and payment required to be made in connection with the later payment, the amount referred to in section 22(1)(a) of this Act shall be reduced by the amount of any relevant payment made in connection with the earlier payment, or, if more than one, the aggregate of those relevant payments.

(3) In relation to the later payment, the compensator shall take the amount of the reduction required by sub-paragraph (2) above to be such as may be specified under paragraph 3(2)(d) above in the certificate of total benefit issued to him in connection with that later payment.

(4) In any case where—
(a) the relevant payment made in connection with an earlier payment is not reflected in the certificate of total benefit in force in relation to a later payment, and
(b) in consequence, the aggregate of the relevant payments made in relation to the later payment and every earlier payment exceeds what it would have been had that relevant payment been so reflected,
the Secretary of State shall pay the intended recipient an amount equal to the excess.

(5) In determining any rights and liabilities in respect of contribution or indemnity, relevant payments shall be treated as damages paid to or for the intended recipient in respect of the accident, injury or disease in question.

Collaboration between compensators

6. (1) This paragraph applies where compensation payments in respect of the same accident, injury or disease fall (or apart from the recoupment provisions would fall) to be made to or in respect of the same victim by two or more compensators.

(2) Where this paragraph applies, any two or more of those compensators may give the Secretary of State notice that they are collaborators in respect of compensation payments in respect of that victim and that accident, injury or disease.

(3) Where such a notice is given and any of the collaborators makes a relevant payment in connection with such a compensation payment, each of the other collaborators shall be treated as if the aggregate amount of relevant payments specified in his certificate of total benefit, as in force at the time of that relevant payment, or in a fresh certificate which does not purport to reflect the payment, were increased by the amount of that payment.

Structured settlements

7. (1) This paragraph applies where—
(a) in final settlement of a person's claim, an agreement is entered into—

        (i) for the making of periodical payments (whether of an income or capital nature) to or in respect of the victim; or
        (ii) for the making of such payments and one or more lump sum payments; and
    (b) apart from this paragraph, those payments would fall to be regarded for the purposes of the recoupment provisions as compensation payments.
    (2) Where this paragraph applies, the recoupment provisions (other than this paragraph) shall have effect on the following assumptions, that is to say—
    (a) the relevant period in the case of the compensator in question shall be taken to end (if it has not previously done so) on the day of settlement;
    (b) the compensator in question shall be taken—
        (i) to have been liable to make on that day a single compensation payment of the amount referred to in section 22(1)(a) of this Act (reduced or increased in accordance with such of the recoupment provisions as would have applied in the case of a payment on that day); and
        (ii) to have made from that single payment a relevant deduction of an amount equal to it; and
    (c) the payments under the agreement referred to in sub-paragraph (1) above shall be taken to be exempt payments.
    (3) The intended recipient shall not by virtue of anything in this paragraph become entitled to be paid any sum, whether by the compensator or the Secretary of State, and if on a review or appeal under paragraph 16 or 18 below it appears that the amount paid by a compensator in pursuance of this paragraph was either greater or less than it ought to have been, then—
    (a) any excess shall be repaid to the compensator instead of to the intended recipient; but
    (b) any deficiency shall be paid to the Secretary of State by the intended recipient.
    (4) Where any further compensation payment falls to be made to or in respect of the victim otherwise than under the agreement in question, sub-paragraph (2)(a) above shall be disregarded for the purpose of determining the end of the relevant period in relation to that further payment.
    (5) In any case where—
    (a) the person making the periodical payments (the 'secondary party') does so in pursuance of arrangements entered into with another (as in a case where an insurance company purchases an annuity for the victim from another such company), and
    (b) apart from those arrangements, that other ('the primary party') would have been regarded as the compensator,
then for the purposes of the recoupment provisions, the primary party shall be regarded as the compensator and the secondary party shall not be so regarded.
    (6) In determining for the purposes of this paragraph whether any periodical payments would fall to be regarded as compensation payments, section 22(4)(a) of this Act shall be disregarded.

(7) In this paragraph 'the day of settlement' means—
   (a) if the agreement referred to in sub-paragraph (1) above is approved by a court, the day on which that approval is given; and
   (b) in any other case, the day on which that agreement is entered into.

Insolvency

8. (1) Where the intended recipient is subject to a bankruptcy order, nothing in the Insolvency Act 1986 shall affect the operation of the recoupment provisions.
(2) Where the estate of the intended recipient is sequestrated, the relevant deduction from the compensation payment shall not form part of the whole estate of the debtor, within the meaning of section 31(8) of the Bankruptcy (Scotland) Act 1985.

Protection of legal aid charges

9. (1) In any case where—
   (a) the compensation payment is subject to any charge under the Legal Aid Act 1974 or the Legal Aid Act 1988, and
   (b) after the making of the relevant deduction, the balance of the compensation payment is insufficient to satisfy that charge,
the Secretary of State shall make such a payment as will secure that the deficiency is made good to the extent of the relevant payment.
(2) Where the Secretary of State makes a payment under this paragraph, then, for the purposes of paragraph 3 above, the amount of the payment shall be treated as increasing the total benefit.
(3) In the application of this paragraph to Scotland, references in sub-paragraph (1) to a charge under the Acts specified shall be construed as references to any provisions of the Legal Aid (Scotland) Act 1986 for the repayment to the Scottish Legal Aid Fund of sums paid by it on behalf of the intended recipient in respect of the proceedings in which the compensation payment is made.

Overpaid benefits

10. In any case where—
   (a) during the relevant period, there has, in respect of the accident, injury or disease, been paid to or for the victim any relevant benefit to which he was not entitled ('the overpaid benefit'), and
   (b) the amount of the relevant payment is such that, after taking account of the rest of the total benefit, there remains an amount which represents the whole or any part of the overpaid benefit,
then, notwithstanding anything in section 53 of the 1986 Act or any regulations under the section, the receipt by the Secretary of State of the relevant payment shall be treated as the recovery of the whole or, as the case may be, that part of the overpaid benefit.

Death

11. In the case of any compensation payment the whole or part of which is made—
   (a) in consequence of an action under the Fatal Accidents Act 1976, or
   (b) in circumstances where, had an action been brought, it would have been brought under that Act, or
   (c) in respect of a liability arising by virtue of section 1 of the Damages (Scotland) Act 1976,

regulations may make provision for estimating or calculating the portion of the payment which is to be regarded as so made for the purposes of section 22(4)(c) or (d) of this Act.

Payments into court

12. (1) Nothing in the recoupment provisions requires a court to make any relevant deduction or payment in connection with money in court.

(2) Where a party to an action makes a payment into court which, had it been paid directly to the other party, would have constituted a compensation payment, the making of that payment shall be regarded for the purposes of the recoupment provisions as the making of a compensation payment, but the compensator—
   (a) may either—
      (i) withhold from such a payment into court an amount equal to the relevant deduction; or
      (ii) make such a payment into court before the certificate of total benefit has been issued to him; and
   (b) shall not become liable to make the relevant payment, or to furnish a certificate of deduction, until he has been notified that the whole or any part of the payment into court has been paid out of court to or for the other party.

(3) Where a person making a payment into court withholds an amount in accordance with sub-paragraph (2)(a)(i) above—
   (a) he shall, at the time when he makes the payment, furnish the court with a certificate of the amount so withheld; and
   (b) the amount paid into court shall be regarded as increased by the amount so certified;

but no person shall be entitled by virtue of this sub-paragraph to the payment out of court of any amount which has not in fact been paid into court.

(4) Where a payment into court is made as mentioned in sub-paragraph (2)(a)(ii) above, the compensator—
   (a) shall apply for the certificate of total benefit no later than the day on which the payment into court is made; and
   (b) shall become liable to make the relevant payment as mentioned in sub-paragraph (2)(b) above, notwithstanding that the relevant deduction has not been made.

(5) Where any such payment into court as is mentioned in sub-paragraph (2) above is accepted by the other party to the action within the initial period, then, as respects the compensator in question, the relevant period shall be taken to have ended on the day on which the payment into court (or, if there were two or more such payments, the last of them) was made; but where the payment into court is not so accepted, then—
    (a) the relevant period as respects that compensator shall end on the day on which he is notified that the payment has been paid out of court to or for that other party; and
    (b) in determining the amount of the relevant payment, that compensator shall be treated as if his payment into court had been made on that day.
(6) In sub-paragraph (5) above 'the initial period' means the period of 21 days following the making of the payment into court (or, if there were two or more such payments, the last of them), but rules of court may make provision varying the length of that period.
(6A) Where a payment into court is paid out wholly to or for the party who made the payment (otherwise than to or for the other party to the action) the making of the payment into court shall cease to be regarded as the making of a compensation payment.
(7) Rules of court may make provision regulating or prescribing the practice and procedure to be followed in relation to such payments into court as are mentioned in sub-paragraph (2) above.
(8) This paragraph does not extend to Scotland.

PART III

Provision of information

13. (1) Any person who is, or is alleged to be, liable in respect of an accident, injury or disease, or any person acting on his behalf, shall furnish the Secretary of State with the prescribed information relating to any person seeking compensation, or in respect of whom compensation is sought, in respect of that accident, injury or disease.
(2) Any person who claims a relevant benefit or who has been in receipt of such a benefit or, if he has died, the personal representatives of such a person, shall furnish the Secretary of State with the prescribed information relating to any accident, injury or disease suffered by that person.
(2A) A person who makes any payment (whether a compensation payment or not) on behalf of himself or another—
    (a) in consequence of any accident, injury or disease suffered, or any damage to property sustained, by any other person, or
    (b) which is referable to any costs, or, in Scotland, expenses, incurred by any such other person by reason of such an accident, injury, disease or damage,
shall, if the Secretary of State so requests him in writing, furnish the Secretary of State with such particulars relating to the size and composition of the payment as may be specified in the request.

(3) Any person—
   (a) who is the employer of a person who suffers or has suffered an accident, injury or disease, or
   (b) who has been the employer of such a person at any time during the relevant period,
shall furnish the Secretary of State with the prescribed information relating to the payment of statutory sick pay in respect of that person.
   (4) In sub-paragraph (3) above 'employer' has the same meaning as it has in Part I of the 1982 Act.
   (5) Any person furnishing information under this paragraph shall do so in the prescribed manner, at the prescribed place and within the prescribed time.

Applications for certificates of total benefit

14. (1) If at any time before he makes the compensation payment in question the compensator applies to the Secretary of State in accordance with paragraph 3 above for a certificate of total benefit relating to the victim in question—
   (a) the Secretary of State shall furnish him with such a certificate before the end of the period of 4 weeks, or such other number of weeks as may be prescribed, following the day on which the application is, or is deemed in accordance with regulations to be, received; and
   (b) any certificate so furnished shall, in particular, specify for the purposes of paragraph 3(2)(a) above a date not earlier than the date of the application.
   (2) Where the Secretary of State furnishes any person with a certificate of total benefit, he shall also provide the information contained in that certificate to the person who appears to him to be the victim in relation to the compensation payment in question.
   (3) The victim may apply to the Secretary of State for particulars of the manner in which any amount, rate or period specified in a certificate of total benefit has been determined.

Liability of compensator unenforceable if certificate not issued within time limit

15. (1) The liability of the compensator to make the relevant deduction and payment relating to the first compensation payment after the default date shall not be enforceable if—
   (a) he has made a request under paragraph 14(1) above which—
      (i) accurately states the prescribed particulars relating to the victim and the accident, injury or disease in question; and
      (ii) specifies the name and address of the person to whom the certificate is to be sent;
   (b) he has in his possession a written acknowledgment, sent to him in accordance with regulations, of the receipt of the request; and
   (c) the Secretary of State does not, within the time limit referred to in paragraph 14(1) above, send the certificate to the person specified in the

request as the person to whom the certificate is to be sent, at the address so specified;
and accordingly, where those liabilities cease to be enforceable, nothing in the recoupment provisions shall prevent the compensator from making that compensation payment.

(2) In any case where—
 (a) the liability to make the relevant deduction and payment becomes unenforceable by virtue of this paragraph, but
 (b) the compensator nevertheless makes that deduction and payment,
he shall be treated for all purposes as if the liability had remained enforceable.

(3) Where the compensator, in reliance on this paragraph, does not make the relevant deduction and payment, then—
 (a) he shall within fourteen days of the default date give the Secretary of State notice of that fact together with such other particulars as may be prescribed; and
 (b) in determining the amount of the relevant deduction and payment to be made in connection with any subsequent compensation payment made by the same or any other compensator, the amount which, apart from this paragraph, would have fallen to be deducted and paid by him shall continue to form part of the total benefit and shall not be treated as if it had been paid.

(4) If, in the opinion of the Secretary of State, circumstances have arisen which adversely affect normal methods of communication—
 (a) he may by order provide that no liability shall become unenforceable by virtue of this paragraph during a specified period not exceeding three months; and
 (b) he may continue any such order in force for further periods not exceeding three months at a time.

(5) In this paragraph 'the default date' means the date on which the time limit mentioned in sub-paragraph (1)(c) above expires.

Review of certificates of total benefit

16. (1) The Secretary of State may review any certificate of total benefit if he is satisfied that it was issued in ignorance of, or was based on a mistake as to, some material fact or that a mistake (whether in computation or otherwise) has occurred in its preparation.

(2) On any such review the Secretary of State may either—
 (a) confirm the certificate, or
 (b) issue a fresh certificate containing such variations as he considers appropriate,
but he shall not so vary the certificate as to increase the total benefit.

(3) In any case where—
 (a) one or more relevant payments have been made, and
 (b) in consequence of a review under this paragraph, it appears that the aggregate amount so paid exceeds the amount that ought to have been paid,

the Secretary of State shall pay the intended recipient an amount equal to the excess.

Appeals

17. (1) An appeal shall lie in accordance with this paragraph against any certificate of total benefit at the instance of the compensator, the victim or the intended recipient, on the ground—
    (a) that any amount, rate or period specified in the certificate is incorrect, or
    (b) that benefit paid or payable otherwise than in consequence of the accident, injury or disease in question has been brought into account.

(2) No appeal shall be brought under this paragraph until—
    (a) the claim giving rise to the compensation payment has been finally disposed of; and
    (b) the relevant payment, or where more than one such payment may fall to be made, the final relevant payment, has been made.

(3) Notwithstanding sub-paragraph (2) above, where—
    (a) an award of damages ("provisional damages") has been made under or by virtue of—
        (i) section 32A(2)(a) of the Supreme Court Act 1981,
        (ii) section 12(2)(a) of the Administration of Justice Act 1982, or
        (iii) section 51(2)(a) of the County Courts Act 1984, and
    (b) the relevant payment or, where more than one such payment falls to be made, the final relevant payment in relation to the provisional damages so awarded has been made,
an appeal may be brought under this paragraph against any certificate of total benefit by reference to which the amount of that relevant payment, or any of those relevant payments, was made.

(4) Regulations may—
    (a) make provision as to the manner in which, and the time within which, appeals under this paragraph are to be brought, and
    (b) make provision for the purpose of enabling any such appeal to be treated as an application for review under paragraph 16 above,
and regulations under paragraph (b) above may, in particular, provide that the circumstances in which such a review may be carried out shall not be restricted to those specified in paragraph 16 above.

(5) If any of the medical questions arises for determination on an appeal under this paragraph, the Secretary of State shall refer that question to a medical appeal tribunal, whose determination shall be binding, for the purposes of the appeal, on any social security appeal tribunal to whom a question is referred under sub-paragraph (7) below.

(6) A medical appeal tribunal, in determining any of the medical questions, shall take into account any decision of any court relating to the same, or any similar, issue arising in connection with the accident, injury or disease in question.

(7) If any question concerning any amount, rate or period specified in the certificate of total benefit arises for determination on an appeal under this paragraph, the Secretary of State shall refer the question to a social

security appeal tribunal, but where any medical questions arising on the appeal have been referred to a medical appeal tribunal—

    (a)   he shall not refer any question to the social security appeal tribunal until he has received the determination of the medical appeal tribunal on the questions referred to them; and

    (b)   he shall notify the social security appeal tribunal of the determinations of the medical appeal tribunal.

(8) On a reference under sub-paragraph (7) above a social security appeal tribunal may either—

    (a)   confirm the amounts, rates and periods specified in the certificate of total benefit; or

    (b)   specify any increases, reductions or other variations which are to be made on the issue of the fresh certificate under sub-paragraph (9) below.

(9) When the Secretary of State has received the determinations of the tribunals on the questions referred to them under sub-paragraphs (5) and (7) above, he shall in accordance with those determinations either—

    (a)   confirm the certificate against which the appeal was brought, or

    (b)   issue a fresh certificate.

(10) Regulations may make provision with respect to the procedure for the reference under this paragraph of questions to medical appeal tribunals or social security appeal tribunals.

(11) An appeal shall lie to a Commissioner at the instance of the Secretary of State, the compensator, the victim or the intended recipient from a decision of a medical appeal tribunal or a social security appeal tribunal under this paragraph on the ground that the decision was erroneous in point of law; and for the purposes of appeals under this sub-paragraph—

    (a)   section 101(5), (5A) and (5B) of the principal Act shall apply in relation to an appeal from the decision of a social security appeal tribunal; and

    (b)   section 112(3) of that Act shall apply in relation to an appeal from the decision of a medical appeal tribunal.

(12) In this paragraph 'the medical questions' means—

    (a)   any question whether, as the result of a particular occurrence, a person suffered an injury, sickness or disease;

    (b)   any question as to the period for which a person suffered any injury, sickness or disease.

Recovery in consequence of an appeal

18. (1) Where it appears, in consequence of an appeal under paragraph 17 above, that the aggregate amount of the relevant payment or payments actually made exceeds the amount that ought to have been paid, the Secretary of State shall pay the intended recipient in amount equal to that excess.

(2) Where it appears, in consequence of such an appeal, that the aggregate amount of the relevant payment or payments actually made is less than the amount that ought to have been paid, the intended recipient shall pay the Secretary of State an amount equal to the deficiency.

(3) Without prejudice to any other method of enforcement, an amount payable under sub-paragraph (2) above may be recovered by deduction from any benefits which are prescribed benefits for the purposes of section 53 of the 1986 Act (recovery of overpayments).

Recovery of relevant payment in cases of default

19.—(1) This paragraph applies in any case where the compensator has made a compensation payment but—
 (a) has not requested a certificate of total benefit in respect of the victim, or
 (b) if he has done so, has not made the relevant payment within the time limit imposed by paragraph 2 above.

(2) Where this paragraph applies, the Secretary of State may—
 (a) if no certificate of total benefit has been issued to the compensator, issue to him such a certificate and a demand for the relevant payment to be made forthwith, or
 (b) if a certificate of total benefit has been issued to the compensator, issue to him a copy of that certificate and such a demand,
and that relevant payment shall, to the extent that it does not exceed the amount of the compensation payment, be recoverable by the Secretary of State from the compensator.

(3) Any amount recoverable under this paragraph shall—
 (a) if the compensator resides or carries on business in England and Wales and a county court so orders, be recoverable by execution issued from the county court or otherwise as if it were payable under an order of that court; or
 (b) if the compensator resides or carries on business in Scotland, be enforced in like manner as an extract registered decree arbitral bearing a warrant for execution issued by the sheriff court of any sheriffdom in Scotland.

(4) A document bearing a certificate which—
 (a) is signed by a person authorised in that behalf by the Secretary of State, and
 (b) states that the document, apart from the certificate, is a record of the amount recoverable under this paragraph,
shall be conclusive evidence that that amount is so recoverable, and a certificate purporting to be signed as aforesaid shall be deemed to be so signed unless the contrary is proved.

(5) Where this paragraph applies in relation to two or more connected compensators, the Secretary of State may proceed against them as if they were jointly and severally liable for an amount equal to the difference between—
 (a) the total benefit determined in accordance with the latest connected certificate of total benefit issued to any of them, and
 (b) the aggregate amount of any connected relevant payments previously made.

(6) Nothing in sub-paragraph (5) above authorises the recovery from any person of an amount in excess of the compensation payment by virtue

of which this paragraph applies to him (or, if there are two or more such payments which are connected, the aggregate amount of those payments).

(7) In sub-paragraphs (5) and (6) above, 'connected' means relating to the same victim and the same accident, injury or disease.

Inspection

20. (1) Section 58 of the 1986 Act (inspection) shall be amended in accordance with the following provisions of this paragraph.

(2) In subsection (2) (powers of inspector to enter, examine and enquire), for sub-paragraph (ii) of paragraph (b) there shall be substituted—

'(ii) for investigating the circumstances in which any accident, injury or disease which has given or may give rise to a claim for industrial injuries benefit, or for any benefit which is a relevant benefit for the purposes of the recoupment provisions, occurred or may have occurred, or was or may have been received or contracted;'.

(3) In paragraph (c) of that subsection, after sub-paragraph (ii) there shall be inserted—

'(iii) a compensation payment or a relevant payment, within the meaning of the recoupment provisions;'.

(4) In subsection (3) (premises which are liable to inspection) after paragraph (c) there shall be inserted—

'(d) any person—

(i) who is the compensator, within the meaning of the recoupment provisions, in relation to any such accident, injury or disease as is referred to in subsection (2)(b)(ii) above, or

(ii) on whose behalf any such compensator has or may have made, or may make, a compensation payment, within the meaning of those provisions,

carries on business or is to be found;'.

(5) In subsection (6) (persons to furnish information required for ascertaining whether certain sums are or have been paid or payable) in paragraph (a), after sub-paragraph (ii), there shall be inserted—

'(iii) any compensation payment or relevant payment, within the meaning of the recoupment provisions;'.

(6) In subsection (7) (persons who are under a duty to provide information) at the end of paragraph (e) there shall be added the words 'or to make any compensation payment or relevant payment, within the meaning of the recoupment provisions'.

(7) After subsection (9) there shall be added—

'(10) In this section 'the recoupment provisions' means section 22 of, and Schedule 4 to, the Social Security Act 1989 (recovery from damages etc. of sums equivalent to benefit paid).'

PART IV

'Persons in Northern Ireland

20A. (1) Where, immediately before making a compensation payment to or in respect of a victim, the compensator—

(a) is not resident and does not have a place of business in Great Britain, but

(b) is resident or has a place of business in Northern Ireland,

the Great Britain provisions shall apply as if at that time he were resident or had a place of business in the relevant part of Great Britain.

(2) Where, immediately before making a Northern Ireland compensation payment to or in respect of a Northern Ireland victim, the Northern Ireland compensator—

(a) is not resident and does not have a place of business in Northern Ireland, but

(b) is resident or has a place of business in any part of Great Britain,

the Northern Ireland provisions shall apply as if at that time he were resident or had a place of business in Northern Ireland.

(3) Where an address in Northern Ireland is the first address notified in writing to the compensator by or on behalf of the victim as his residence (or, if the victim has died, by or on behalf of the intended recipient as the victim's last residence) then—

(a) the compensator shall apply, as a Northern Ireland compensator, for a Northern Ireland certificate in accordance with the Northern Ireland provisions (and shall not make any separate application for a certificate of total benefit);

(b) any Northern Ireland certificate which is issued to the compensator in relation to the victim and the accident, injury or disease in question—

(i) shall contain a statement that it is to be treated as including a certificate of total benefit so issued by the Secretary of State and that any relevant payment required to be made to him by reference thereto is to be paid to the Northern Ireland Department as his agent; and

(ii) shall be taken to include such a certificate of total benefit; and

(c) any payment made by the compensator to the Northern Ireland Department in pursuance of such a Northern Ireland certificate shall be applied—

(i) first towards discharging his liability under the Northern Ireland provisions, and

(ii) then, as respects any remaining balance, towards discharging his liability under the Great Britain provisions,

in respect of the relevant victim and that accident, injury or disease.

(4) Where an address in any part of Great Britain is the first address notified in writing to the Northern Ireland compensator by or on behalf of the Northern Ireland victim as his residence (or, if the Northern Ireland victim has died, by or on behalf of the Northern Ireland intended recipient as the Northern Ireland victim's last residence) then—

(a) the Northern Ireland compensator shall apply, as a compensator, for a certificate of total benefit in accordance with the Great Britain provisions (and shall not make any separate application for a Northern Ireland certificate);

(b) any certificate of total benefit which is issued to the Northern Ireland compensator in relation to the Northern Ireland victim and the accident, injury or disease in question—
    (i) shall contain a statement that it is to be treated as including a Northern Ireland certificate so issued by the Northern Ireland Department and that any Northern Ireland relevant payment required to be made to that Department by reference thereto is to be paid to the Secretary of State as its agent; and
    (ii) shall be taken to include such a Northern Ireland certificate; and
(c) any payment made by the Northern Ireland compensator to the Secretary of State in pursuance of such a certificate shall be applied—
    (i) first towards discharging his liability under the Great Britain provisions, and
    (ii) then, as respects any remaining balance, towards discharging his liability under the Northern Ireland provisions,
in respect of the relevant victim and the accident, injury or disease.

(5) For the purposes of sub-paragraph (1) above, 'the relevant part of Great Britain', in relation to a compensator, means—
    (a) if the compensator has been notified in writing—
        (i) by or on behalf of the victim, or
        (ii) where the victim has died, by or on behalf of the intended recipient,
that the victim is or was at any time resident at an address in any part of Great Britain, that part of Great Britain (or, if more than one such notification has been given, the part in which he was so notified that the victim was most recently so resident); or
    (b) in any other case, such a part of Great Britain as the Secretary of State may determine in accordance with regulations.

(6) In this paragraph—
'the Great Britain provisions' means the recoupment provisions, other than this paragraph;
'Northern Ireland certificate' means a certificate of total benefit, within the meaning of the Northern Ireland provisions;
'Northern Ireland compensation payment' means a compensation payment, within the meaning of the Northern Ireland provisions;
'Northern Ireland compensator' means a compensator, within the meaning of the Northern Ireland provisions;
'the Northern Ireland Department' has the same meaning as it has in the principal Act;
'the Northern Ireland intended recipient' means the intended recipient, within the meaning of the Northern Ireland provisions, in relation to a Northern Ireland compensation payment;
'the Northern Ireland provisions' means any legislation corresponding to the recoupment provisions (other than this paragraph) and having effect in Northern Ireland;
'Northern Ireland relevant payment' means a relevant payment, within the meaning of the Northern Ireland provisions;

'Northern Ireland victim' means a person who is the victim, within the meaning of the Northern Ireland provisions, in relation to a Northern Ireland compensation payment;
'the relevant victim' means the person who is the victim or the Northern Ireland victim (or both), as the case may be.
   (7)   This paragraph extends to Northern Ireland.'

Foreign compensators: duties of intended recipient

21. (1) Where, immediately before the making of the compensation payment, the compensator is not resident and does not have a place of business in any part of the United Kingdom, any deduction, payment or other thing which would, apart from this paragraph, fall to be made or done under the recoupment provisions by the compensator shall instead be made or done by the intended recipient and references to the compensator shall be construed accordingly.
   (2)   The Secretary of State may by regulations make such provision as he considers expedient for the purpose of modifying the recoupment provisions in their application in such a case.

Modification of Law Reform (Personal Injuries) Act 1948

22. (1) In section 2 of the Law Reform (Personal Injuries) Act 1948, in subsection (1) (which requires that, in assessing damages, half of certain benefits shall be brought into account against loss of profits or earnings)—
   (a)   after the word 'contract),' there shall be inserted the words 'where this section applies';
   (b)   for the words from 'against any loss' to 'from the injuries' there shall be substituted the words 'against them'; and
   (c)   for the words from 'therefrom' onwards there shall be substituted the words 'from the injuries in respect of—
      (a)   any of the relevant benefits, within the meaning of section 22 of the Social Security Act 1989, or
      (b)   any corresponding benefits payable in Northern Ireland,
for the five years beginning with the time when the cause of action accrued.'
   (2)   After that subsection there shall be inserted—
   '(1A) This section applies in any case where the amount of the damages that would have been awarded apart from any reduction under subsection (1) above is less than the sum for the time being prescribed under paragraph 4(1) of Schedule 4 to the Social Security Act 1989 (recoupment of benefit: exception for small payments).'
   (3)   Subsection (2) of that section (disregard of increase for constant attendance) shall cease to have effect.

Modification of Bankruptcy (Scotland) Act 1985

23. In section 31 of the Bankruptcy (Scotland) Act 1985 (vesting of debtor's estate at date of sequestration) in subsection (8) after the words 'subsection (9) below' there shall be inserted the words 'and to paragraph 8(2) of Schedule 4 to the Social Security Act 1989.'

'*Interest on damages: reductions in respect of relevant payments*

24. In assessing the amount of interest payable in respect of an award of damages, the amount of the award shall be treated as reduced by a sum equal to the amount of the relevant payment (if any) required to be made in connection with the payment of the damages and—

    (a) in England and Wales, if both special and general damages are awarded, any such reductions shall be treated as made first against the special damages and then, as respects any remaining balance, against the general damages; and

    (b) in Scotland, if damages are awarded both for patrimonial loss and for solatium, any such reductions shall be treated as made first against the damages for patrimonial loss and then, as respects any remaining balance, against the damages for solatium.'

Social Security Act 1990, s. 7

Law Reform (Personal Injuries) Act 1948 (c. 41)

7. The enactments specified in Schedule 1 to this Act shall have effect with the amendments specified in that Schedule.

Comment

The schedule amends s. 22(3) and sch. 4 of the 1989 Act as shown here and in Chapter 2. Additional minor amendments are made to the Law Reform (Personal Injuries) Act 1948 and s. 33(6) of the 1989 Act. Those provisions are not reproduced here.

Courts and Legal Services Act 1990

There are many changes of procedure and substance contained within this legislation which may dramatically alter the shape and nature of civil litigation and its conduct. Most of these will have particular import in the conduct of personal injury litigation, but fall outside the scope of this review. It may be briefly noted that the Act removes all restrictions on rights of audience in certain county court proceedings, enabling lay representatives to appear on behalf of litigants; establishes new machinery which will enable solicitors to gain new rights of audience and barristers to gain the right to conduct civil litigation, and heralds new classes of advocate and litigator to become qualified and appear in the courts; removes the current restrictions on the use of conditional agreements where the client enters into an agreement that if the case is lost, the lawyer will take no fee. By far the most important provision for current purposes, however, relates to the reallocation of business between courts. From July 1991 personal injury actions below £50,000 will be required to be commenced in the county court. Other reforms which are likely to come into effect on the same date include:

    (a)   the introduction of interest to county court awards with an order to that effect being made under the County Courts Act 1984, s. 74. No special application for interest in the particulars of claim will be needed and a defendant who is discharging the judgment by instalments will become liable to interest only if he or she falls into arrears;

    (b)   the High Court rule which allows the plaintiff to choose venue will be extended to the county court — defended actions not issued out of the defendant's home court will be automatically transferred there if for a liquidated sum. In relation to unliquidated sums the defendant can apply for transfer to his or her local court;

    (c)   a defendant who admits a claim but asks for time to pay will be required to communicate this directly to the plaintiff, who will then either certify to the court that he or she is entering judgment or request a hearing;

    (d)   registrars (district judges) will be relieved of the burden of dealing with disposals, variations of orders, suspensions of warrants of execution, attachment of earnings orders, and consent orders. This work will be done by court staff;

    (e)   the county court small claims jurisdiction is set to rise;

    (f)   plaintiff's solicitors will be able to serve summonses by post.

2

STATUTORY INSTRUMENTS

Social Security (Recoupment) Regulations 1990
(SI 1990 No. 332 (as amended by Social Security (Recoupment) Amendment Regulations SI 1990 No. 1558)

Came into force, 2 April 1990
These rules elaborate the scheme established by the Social Security Act 1989, s. 22 and sch. 4 (as amended), which was discussed in Chapter 1. Regulation 2 specifies the 'relevant' payments in respect of which full deduction must be made. Where a plaintiff has received any of these benefits then the clawback provisions will operate. The benefits are:

(a) attendance allowance;
(b) disablement benefit (including disablement pensions) payable in accordance with ss. 57–63 of the Social Security Act 1975;
(c) family credit;
(d) income support under Part II of the Social Security Act 1986, including personal expenses addition, special transitional additions and transitional addition as defined in the Income Support (Transitional) Regulations 1987;
(e) invalidity pension and allowance;
(f) mobility allowance;
(g) benefits payable under schemes made under the Old Cases Act (the Industrial Injuries and Diseases (Old Cases) Act 1975);
(h) reduced earnings allowance;
(i) retirement allowance;
(j) severe disablement allowance;
(k) sickness benefit;
(l) statutory sick pay;

(m) unemployment benefit;

(n) any increase in any of these benefits payable in accordance with the Social Security Acts 1975 to 1989 or the Old Cases Act or in accordance with any regulations, Orders in Council, or order or scheme thereunder;

(o) in respect of invalidity pension and allowance, severe disablement allowance, sickness benefit and unemployment benefit; reference to any payment includes reference to any income support paid with each of those benefits on the same instrument of payment; for these purposes, income support includes personal expenses addition, special transitional additions and transitional addition as defined in the Income Support (Transitional) Regulations 1987.

Regulation 4 (as amended by Social Security (Recoupment) Amendment Regulations 1990) elaborates upon those payments which are to be regarded as exempt payments for the purposes of s. 22. These include:

(a) payments made out of property held for the purpose of the charitable Macfarlane Trust established partly out of funds provided by the Secretary of State to the Haemophilia Society for the relief of poverty or distress among those suffering from haemophilia;

(b) payments made by British Coal under the NCB Pneumoconiosis Compensation Scheme;

(c) certain payments made for sensorineural hearing loss;

(d) any contractual amount paid to an employee by an employer in respect of a day of incapacity for work;

(e) any payment made from the Macfarlane (Special Payments) Trust;

(f) any payment made under the National Health Service (Injury Benefits) Regulations 1974 or the National Health Service (Scotland) (Injury Benefits) Regulations 1974.

Regulation 5 specifies what information the person who is or who is alleged to be liable in respect of an accident, injury or disease is required to provide to the Secretary of State (name and address of the person seeking compensation; date of birth, national insurance number — if known; where the liability arises or is alleged to arise;

the nature of the accident, injury or disease; and — if known — whether at the time of the accident, injury or disease, the person claiming compensation was employed under a contract of service, and if so, his or her employer, that person's address and that person's payroll number). Further regulations provide for information which must be supplied by the victim and, if applicable, the employer.

Social Security (Recoupment) Regulations 1990
(SI 1990 No. 322) (as amended by Social Security (Recoupment) Amendment Regulations 1990 (SI 1990 No. 1558)

PART I   GENERAL

1 Citation, commencement and interpretation
(1) These Regulations may be cited as the Social Security (Recoupment) Regulations 1990 and shall come into force for the purposes of this regulation and regulations 5, 6, 7, 8 and 16 on 2nd April 1990;
for the purposes of regulations 2, 9, 10, 13 and 15 on 9th July 1990;
and for all other purposes on 3rd September 1990.
(2)   In these Regulations—
'the 1989 Act' means the Social Security Act 1989;
'Schedule 4' means Schedule 4 to the 1989 Act; and
'the Compensation Recovery Unit' means the Compensation Recovery Unit of the Department of Social Security at Reyrolle Building, Hebburn, Tyne and Wear.
(3)   In these Regulations, unless the context otherwise requires, a reference—
   (a) to a numbered regulation is to the regulation in these Regulations bearing that number; and
   (b) in a regulation to a numbered paragraph is to the paragraph in that regulation bearing that number.

2 Relevant benefits
(1)   The following benefits are relevant benefits for the purposes of section 22 of the 1989 Act—
   (a)   attendance allowance,
   (b)   disablement benefit (including disablement pensions) payable in accordance with sections 57 to 63 of the principal Act,
   (c)   family credit,
   (d)   income support, under Part II of the Social Security Act 1986, including personal expenses addition, special transitional additions and transitional addition as defined in the Income Support (Transitional) Regulations 1987,
   (e)   invalidity pension and allowance;
   (f)   mobility allowance,

(g) benefits payable under schemes made under the Old Cases Act,
(h) reduced earnings allowance,
(i) retirement allowance,
(j) severe disablement allowance,
(k) sickness benefit,
(l) statutory sick pay,
(m) unemployment benefit,
(n) any increase in any of the benefits mentioned above payable in accordance with the Social Security Acts 1975 to 1989 or the Old Cases Act or with any regulations, Order in Council, order or scheme made thereunder.

(2) In paragraph (1) references to, respectively, invalidity pension and allowance, severe disablement allowance, sickness benefit and unemployment benefit include also a reference to any income support paid with each of those benefits on the same instrument of payment, and for this purpose, income support includes personal expenses addition, special transitional additions and transitional addition as defined in the Income Support (Transitional) Regulations 1987.

PART II   BENEFITS AND PAYMENTS

3 Small benefits

(1) A person shall be exempted from liability to make the relevant deduction or the relevant payment where the amount of the compensation payment in question, or the aggregate amount of 2 or more connected compensation payments, does not exceed £2,500.

(2) Where an amount has been deducted and paid to the Secretary of State which, by virtue of paragraph (1), ought not to have been so deducted and paid, the Secretary of State—
  (a) Where he is satisfied that the whole of the amount ought to have been paid to the intended recipient, shall pay the whole of that amount to that person; or
  (b) Where he is not so satisfied, shall either pay the whole of the amount to the compensator or pay to the compensator that part of the amount which he would have been entitled to retain and to the intended recipient that part which he would have been entitled to receive had the amount not been so deducted and paid.

4 Exempt benefits

The following payments shall be exempt payments for the purposes of section 22 of the 1989 Act—
  (a) any payment made out of property held for the purpose of the charitable trust called the Macfarlane Trust and established partly out of funds provided by the Secretary of State to the Haemophilia Society for the relief of poverty or distress among those suffering from haemophilia;
  (b) any compensation payment made by British Coal in accordance with the NCB Pneumoconiosis Compensation Scheme set out in the Schedule to an agreement made on the 13th September 1974 between the National Coal Board, the National Union of Mine Workers, the National

Association of Colliery Overmen Deputies and Shot-firers and the British Association of Colliery Management;
 (c) any payment made to the victim in respect of sensorineural hearing loss where the loss is less than 50 db in one or both ears; and
 (d) any contractual amount paid to an employee by an employer of his in respect of a day of incapacity for work.
 (e) any payment made from the Macfarlane (Special Payments) Trust established on 29th January 1990 partly out of funds provided by the Secretary of State for the benefit of certain persons suffering from haemophilia; and
 (f) any payment made under the National Health Service (Injury Benefits) Regulations 1974 or the National Health Service (Scotland) (Injury Benefits) Regulations 1974.

PART III   ADMINISTRATION AND ADJUDICATION

5   Information to be provided by compensator

A person who is, or is alleged to be, liable in respect of an accident, injury or disease, or any person acting on his behalf, shall furnish the Secretary of State with the following information in respect of that accident, injury or disease—
 (a) the full name and the address of any person seeking compensation or in respect of whom compensation is sought;
 (b) where known the date of birth or the national insurance number of that person, or both if both are known;
 (c) where the liability arises, or is alleged to arise, in respect of—
   (i) an accident or injury, the date of the accident or injury; or
   (ii) a disease, the date the disease was diagnosed;
 (d) the nature of the accident, injury or disease; and
 (e) where known, whether at the time of the accident or injury or diagnosis of the disease, the person was employed under a contract of service, and if he was, the name and address of his employer at that time and the person's payroll number.

6   Information to be provided by victim

(1) A person who claims (whether on behalf of himself or another) a relevant benefit or has been in receipt of such a benefit, shall furnish the Secretary of State with such of the following information relating to any accident, injury or disease the victim has suffered as the Secretary of State requests—
 (a) whether the accident, injury or disease resulted from any action taken by another person, or from any failure of another person to act, and if so, the full name and address of that other person;
 (b) whether he has claimed or may claim a compensation payment, and if so, the full name and the address of the person against whom the claim was or may be made;
 (c) the amount of any compensation payment and the date on which it was made;

(d) the relevant benefit claimed, the date from which benefit was first claimed and the amount of the benefit received in the period beginning with that date and ending with the date the information is sent;

(e) in the case of a person who has received or is entitled to receive statutory sick pay during the relevant period, the name and address of any employer who is or was liable to make these payments to him during the relevant period and the dates the employment with that employer began and ended; and

(f) any changes in the medical diagnosis relating to the condition arising from the accident, injury or disease.

(2) In this regulation, 'person' includes a deceased person's personal representative.

7 Information to be provided by employer

Any person—

(a) who is the employer of a person who suffers or has suffered an accident, injury or disease, or

(b) who has been an employer of such a person at any time during the relevant period,

shall furnish the Secretary of State with such of the following information relating to the payment of statutory sick pay as the Secretary of State requests—

(i) the amount of any statutory sick pay he is liable to pay or has paid to the victim since the first day of the relevant period;

(ii) the date the liability first arose and the rate at which statutory sick pay is or was payable;

(iii) the date that such liability terminated or is likely to terminate; and

(iv) the causes of the incapacity for work during any periods of entitlement to statutory sick pay.

8 Sending information

A person who furnishes the Secretary of State with information shall do so by sending it in writing to the Compensation Recovery Unit not later than 14 days after—

(a) where he is a person to whom regulation 5 applies, the date he receives a claim for compensation from the victim in respect of the accident, injury or disease;

(b) where he is a person to whom regulation 6 or 7 applies, the date the Secretary of State requests the information from him.

9 Particulars to be stated before liability of compensator becomes enforceable

The following particulars are prescribed for the purposes of paragraph 15(1)(a)(i) of Schedule 4 (particulars to be stated before liability of compensator becomes unenforceable)—

(a) the full name of the victim together with his address, and either his date of birth or national insurance number or both if both are known,

(b) unless already furnished to the Secretary of State in accordance with regulation 5—

(i) where the liability arises or is alleged to arise in respect of an accident or injury, the date of that accident or injury, or where it arises or is alleged to arise in respect of a disease, the date the disease was diagnosed;
(ii) the nature of the accident, injury or disease; and
(iii) where known, whether at the time of the accident or injury or the diagnosis of the disease the victim was employed under a contract of service, and if he was, the name and address of his employer at that time and the person's payroll number.

10 Acknowledgement of compensator's request
Where the compensator requests a certificate of total benefit in accordance with paragraph 15(1)(a) of Schedule 4, the Secretary of State shall send to the compensator, as soon as reasonably practicable, a written acknowledgement of the receipt of the request stating the day on which the request was received.

11 Appeals
(1) Any appeal against a certificate of total benefit shall be in writing and shall be made by sending or delivering it to the Compensation Recovery Unit
 (a) not later than 3 months after the date the compensator made the relevant payment; or
 (b) where the certificate was reviewed by the Secretary of State in accordance with Regulation 13 not later than 3 months from the date the certificate is confirmed, or as the case may be, a fresh certificate issued.
(2) Any appeal under this regulation shall contain particulars of the grounds on which it is made.
(3) Where an earlier compensation payment has been made and subsequently one or more later payments are made to or in respect of the same victim in respect of the same accident, injury or disease (whether by the same or an other compensator), the date referred to in paragraph (1)(a) is the date of the last of those later payments.
(4) The time for making an appeal may be extended for special reasons by the chairman of the tribunal to which the appeal is referred, even though the time limit may have already expired.
(5) Any application for an extension of time under paragraph (4) shall be made in writing and shall be determined by the chairman.
(6) An application under paragraph (4) for an extension of time which has been refused shall not be renewed.
(7) Where it appears to the chairman of the tribunal to whom the appeal was referred that the appeal gives insufficient particulars to enable the question at issue to be determined, he may require the person making the appeal to furnish such further particulars as may reasonably be required.

12 Withdrawal of appeals
A person who has made an appeal under regulation 11 may withdraw that appeal—

(a) before the hearing begins by giving notice in writing of his intention to withdraw the appeal to the Appeal Tribunal to whom the appeal was made and with the consent in writing of the Secretary of State;

(b) after the hearing has begun and before the determination is made, with the leave of the chairman of the Appeal Tribunal.

13 Review

The Secretary of State may treat any appeal as an application for review under paragraph 16 of Schedule 4, notwithstanding that the certificate of total benefit was not issued in ignorance of or based on a mistake as to some material fact or that a mistake (whether in computation or otherwise) has not occurred in its preparation.

14 Benefits exceed compensation

Where, after making the relevant deduction from the compensation payment, there is no balance remaining for payment to the intended recipient, any reference in Schedule 4 to the making of the compensation payment shall be construed as a reference to the acceptance by the intended recipient of an offer in respect of his claim against the compensator.

15 Foreign compensators

Where immediately before the making of a compensation payment, the compensator is not resident and does not have a place of business in Great Britain, then these Regulations shall be modified in their application to the intended recipient in accordance with the following provisions—

(a) regulation 5 shall apply with the additional requirement that the intended recipient supply the Secretary of State with the name of the compensator and his address; and

(b) regulation 9 shall apply with the additional requirement that he supply the Secretary of State with details of—

(i) the amount of the compensation paid to him, and

(ii) whether that payment represents the final payment in respect of the accident, injury or disease.

16 Transitional provisions and saving

(1) A compensator who may make a compensation payment after 2nd September 1990 in respect of an accident, injury or disease which occurred on or after 1st January 1989 but before 2nd April 1990, shall so inform the Secretary of State as soon as reasonably practicable.

(2) Where an accident or injury occurred or a disease was diagnosed before 1st January 1989 and a compensation payment in respect of that accident, injury or disease is or may be made after 2nd September 1990, then

(a) the provisions of section 2 of the Law Reform (Personal Injuries) Act 1948 shall apply to that payment as though the amendment made to it in paragraph 22 of Schedule 4 to the 1989 Act, had not been enacted, and

(b) the payment shall be calculated as if section 22(6) of that Act had not been enacted.

Rules of the Supreme Court (Amendment No. 2) 1990
(SI 1990 No. 1689 (L16) rr. 1, 18, 21, 31)

Came into force, 1 October 1990
These rules provide, *inter alia*, for the amendment of RSC ord. 22 r. 5. Rule 18 of these amendments adds, after the present ord. 22 r. 5 a new rule, r. 5(2). The effect of this is that where a payment into court has been made within the terms of the recoupment provisions of the 1989 Social Security Act (as amended) and an application is made for the money remaining in court to be paid out, the court may treat the money in court as being reduced by a sum equivalent to any further relevant benefits (as defined, see s. 22(3) and Recoupment Regulations discussed above) paid to the plaintiff since the date of payment into court. The court may then direct that the payment out is made in accordance with this deemed further reduction, thus ensuring that the plaintiff enjoys no element of double recovery from monies paid into court.

Rules 21 and 31 make minor and consequential amendments.

The Rules of the Supreme Court (Amendment No. 2) 1990
(SI 1990 No. 1689 (L. 16))

1. Citation and commencement
(1) These Rules may be cited as the Rules of the Supreme Court (Amendment No. 2) 1990 and shall come into force on 1st October 1990.
(2) In these Rules, an Order referred to by number means the Order so numbered in the Rules of the Supreme Court 1965 and a reference to Appendix A or B is a reference to Appendix A or B to those Rules.

18. Recovery of social security benefits
Order 22, rule 5 shall be amended as follows—
    (a) the present text shall stand as paragraph (1);
    (b) after paragraph (1), there shall be inserted the following new paragraph—
'(2) In a case where a payment into court has been made as mentioned in paragraph 12(2) of Schedule 4 to the Social Security Act 1989 and an application is made for the money remaining in court to be paid out, the court may treat the money in court as being reduced by a sum equivalent to any further relevant benefits (within the meaning of section 22(3) of that Act) paid to the plaintiff since the date of payment into court and direct payment out accordingly.'.

20. Order 62, rule 9 shall be amended as follows—

(a) the present text, as amended in accordance with (b) below, shall stand as paragraph (1);

(b) in paragraph (1)(d) there shall be inserted, after the words 'provided that', the words ', except in a case to which paragraph (2) applies,';

(c) after paragraph (1) there shall be inserted the following new paragraph—

'(2) This paragraph applies to a case where the party making the offer has applied for, but has not yet received, a certificate of total benefit given in accordance with Schedule 4 to the Social Security Act 1989; but this paragraph shall not apply with respect to any time after 7 days after that party has received the certificate.'.

21. Form No. 23 in Appendix A shall be amended by inserting, before the words 'Dated the   day of   19 .', the following paragraph—

'[The defendant has withheld from this payment into court the sum of £   in accordance with paragraph 12(2)(a)(i) of Schedule 4 to the Social Security Act 1989.]'.

31. Minor corrections

For Table A (Basic Costs) In Part I of Appendix 3 to Order 62 there shall be substituted the following—

A. Basic Costs

	Amount to be allowed in cases under following sub-paragraphs of paragraph 1 of this Appendix		
	(a) £p	(b) £p	(c) £p
If the amount recovered is—			
not less than £600 but less than £2,000—			
(i) where the writ was served by post	50.00	66.00	116.00
(ii) where the writ was served on the defendant personally	56.00	71.00	121.00
not less than £2,000 but less than £3,000—			
(i) where the writ was served by post	56.00	73.00	121.00
(ii) where the writ was served on the defendant personally	66.00	77.00	127.00
not less than £3,000	73.00	105.00	150.00

Rules of the Supreme Court (Amendment No. 4) 1989
(SI 1989 No. 2427 (L. 20))
County Court (Amendment No. 4) Rules 1989
(SI 1989 No. 2426 (L. 19))

Came into force, 5 February 1990 or 4 June 1990
These rules announced a major shake up in the way in which civil litigation will be handled. The aim of the reforms which the rules introduced is to provide for a more open, negotiated approach to the disposal of civil claims. The rules are a consequence of the review of the system undertaken by the Lord Chancellor's Civil Justice Review Body (Cm 394), and most of the changes came into effect from 5 February 1990 or 4 June 1990. Personal injury cases are identified for particular treatment under the revised system.

There are four major changes to personal injury litigation. Plaintiffs will be required to produce extra documents when serving a statement of claim or summons; automatic directions are extended to the county court; provisional damages are introduced to that jurisdiction and finally the High Court may order split trials of its own motion. Each of these reforms deserves separate consideration.

Additional documents
From 4 June 1990 it has been necessary for a plaintiff, when serving a statement of claim, to include a medical report of his or her injuries and a statement which gives full particulars of any special damages claimed. This replaces the previous practice of simultaneous exchange of experts' reports. It may be that this will give some marginal advantage to the defendant, in being able to cut his or her evidence according to the shape of the plaintiff's coat. The second reform, of detailed special damages claimed, actually adds little to the previous practice. The new requirement appears to envisage that a plaintiff will specify in more detail the nature of the special damages claimed, but as plaintiffs had already to claim any special damages in their statement, this change may be more apparent than real. The rules specify that the statement should include an estimate of any future expenses and losses, including loss of earnings and pension rights, whereas such calculations were previously made shortly before trial. Otherwise the rules are vague as to the precise content of the statement.

Automatic directions

High Court actions for personal injuries have benefitted from the availability of automatic directions since 1980. The extension of that facility to the county court reproduces in almost exact form the High Court practice, and replaces statutorily what has informally taken the place of the pretrial review in many courts (see now CCR ord. 17 r. 11). Automatic directions take effect on close of pleadings, and the plaintiff's claim is automatically struck out if he or she fails to apply for a hearing to be fixed within 15 months of the deemed close of proceedings (i.e., 14 days after the delivery of defence or 28 days after delivery of defence with counterclaim). Additionally, the automatic directions provide for:

(a) discovery within 14 days with inspection 7 days thereafter;

(b) except with leave or consent no expert evidence to be adduced unless the substance of the evidence has been disclosed in the form of a written report within 10 weeks of the deemed close of pleadings;

(c) where not agreed otherwise, expert evidence to be limited to two medical and one non-medical witness for each side;

(d) photographs, sketch plans and the police report (for which there is a new scale of fees) to be receivable in evidence at trial and agreed, if possible;

(e) plaintiff to apply for hearing within six months of deemed close, the request to be accompanied by a note, agreed if possible, giving an estimate of the length of the trial and the number of witnesses to be called;

(f) an increase from 14 to 21 days of the minimum notice of the hearing to be given by the court to the parties.

Further or different directions may be applied for by either party where they feel that this would be appropriate.

Provisional damages

The unavailability of provisional damages in the county court has been regarded as a 'procedural spanner' in the workings of the civil justice system. They provide for the unusual case in which there is a real danger that a plaintiff will at some future time suffer further deterioration in his or her medical condition as the result of a

STATUTORY INSTRUMENTS

personal injury (or a prescribed disease) which would leave them seriously undercompensated if the usual one-off award were the final payment. The system has worked well since its 1985 introduction to the High Court and this lacuna in the county court armoury was the reason given by the Court of Appeal in *Kennedy* v *Bowater Containers Ltd* [1990] 2 WLR 84 for refusing to transfer a case to the minor court where provisional damages had been claimed and which could only be awarded if the case remained within the High Court.

Split trials

Under the new rules the court may itself take the initiative to order split trials on issues of liability and quantum, whereas previously this was available only on the application of one of the parties. Masters and district registrars may now initiate the split, which was an opportunity taken rarely by litigants, even though in cases where the medical prognosis of the plaintiff's condition was going to take some time to be properly identified, trial as to liability while events remained fresh could be of particular advantage. Any party who objects to the initiative taken by the court has 14 days within which to apply to have the order set aside.

The rules also introduce reform to service of proceedings (where issued after 4 June 1990 these must be served within four months rather than the old limit of one year); exchange of witness statements (county courts now have a parallel power to that granted to the High Court since 1986 to order exchange of the statements of those witnesses whom they intend to call); and the administration of interrogatories. These matters are more fully dealt with in *Blackstone's Annual Update 1991 — Civil Litigation*.

Civil Legal Aid (Assessment of Resources) Regulations 1989
(SI 1989 No. 338)
Civil Legal Aid (Assessment of Resources) (Amendment) Regulations 1990
(SI 1990 No. 484)

Came into force, 2 April 1990
Under these rules, children under the age of 16 will, for the first time, be assessed on the basis of their own means for legal aid purposes, rather than on those of their parents. The amendments

increased the specified eligibility limits, provided for the disregard of certain capital sums and made other allowances in assessing entitlement to civil legal aid. This is expected to have significant implications for personal injury and medical negligence litigation involving minors. These reforms may bring fundamental changes to birth injury cases, especially those involving brain injury. While it will still be necessary to convince the Legal Aid Board that there is a reasonable chance of a successful action, some firms of solicitors who specialise in this sort of litigation, or who handle a large number of claims on an annual basis, have engaged the full time services of a medical expert to carry out the preliminary investigations, and the detailed and complex work which that involves, in order to increase the likelihood of their clients bringing a successful action. Proceedings have already been initiated by children involved in child abuse allegations in the Cleveland affair against paediatricians involved in diagnosing suspected abuse.

Fixed Costs
Rules of the Supreme Court (Amendment) 1990
(SI 1990 No. 492)
County Court (Amendment) Rules 1990
(SI 1990 No. 516)

TABLE: New Law Journal, 23 March 1990, p. 396

High Court fixed costs

claim and mode of service	14 days	default	Ord 14
£600—under 12,000			
postal	£50.00	£60.00	£116.00
personal	£56.00	£71.00	£121.00
£2,000—under £3,000			
postal	£56.00	£73.00	£121.00
personal	£66.00	£77.00	£127.00
£3,000 plus			
postal and personal	£73.00	£105.00	£150.00

Add writ fee to above or appropriate plaint fee if less than £3,000 recovered

additional defendant
£600—under £3,000	£7.75
£3,000 plus	£10.00

substituted service
£600—under £3,000	£18.00
£3,000 plus	£39.00

Order 14 affidavit of service of summons
£600—under £3,000	£13.00
£3,000 plus	£15.00

County court fixed costs on summons

Claim		
over £25—£250	NSS	£22.50
	SS	£25.25
over £250—£600	NSS	£30.00
	SS	£35.50
over £600—£2,000	NSS	£50.50
	SS	£56.00
over £2,000	NSS	£55.00
	SS	£60.00

NSS = non-solicitor service
SS = solicitor service

County court fixed costs on judgments etc.

type	over £25—£600	over £600—£3,000	over £3,000
by default	£8.00	£15.00	£16.50
by acceptance	£14.00	£29.50	£34.50
disposal	£19.00	£37.50	£44.50
no answer on fixed date action	£28.00	£41.75	£52.00
on warrant of execution		£1.60	

County court assessed costs

lower scale	£42.00—£65.00
scale 1	£46.50—£118.00
scale 2	£73.00—£443.00
scale 3	£106.00—£534.00

Road Traffic Accidents (Payments for Treatment) Order 1990
(SI 1990 No. 1364)

Came into force, 1 August 1990
This order increased the emergency treatment charge from £15 to £18.50. The driver of a vehicle on a road who causes bodily or fatal injury, whether with fault or not, must meet the emergency treatment bill (Road Traffic Act 1988, s. 158). His or her insurers will indemnify without prejudice to the no claims bonus and payment can be claimed back from the wrongdoer.

3

CASES

Personal injury cases fall into three distinct groups dealing with issues of liability, damages and practice and procedure. That natural division is adopted here.

Liability

Jones v Chief Constable of South Yorkshire
[1990] NLJ 1717

Queen's Bench Division (Hidden J)

Subject matter: Nervous shock caused by television transmission.

In what is possibly the most significant High Court decision of 1990, Hidden J was called upon to determine the ambit of negligence liability following the Hillsborough Stadium tragedy. This case was brought by 16 plaintiffs as representative of some 150 who had suffered psychiatric illness in the aftermath of that tragedy in which 95 spectators were crushed to death following an apparent failure of ground supervision and crowd control at a major sporting event. The match was televised and the events in which the deaths occurred were broadcast as they happened. The plaintiffs all had friends or relatives at the match, 13 of whom were killed and two injured. Four of the plaintiffs were at the stadium and were eye-witnesses of the unfolding events; one heard the events being broadcast on the radio, ten saw what was happening on television, and one heard about what had happened and saw a subsequent televised news broadcast. All brought an action against the Chief Constable of the force charged with supervising the crowd on match day. The defendant admitted breach of duty towards the dead and injured and accepted that the plaintiffs had suffered psychiatric illness caused by their awareness of the events. However, he sought to deny liability on the ground that he did not owe them a duty of care.

Held
(1) The class of persons entitled to recover for psychiatric illness caused by a negligent act extends not only to a parent and spouse (as in *McLoughlin* v *O'Brian* [1982] 2 WLR 982) but also to a brother or sister of the victim of negligence, but not to any other relations of the victim, such as an uncle, a grandfather or a brother-in-law, all of which categories were represented in the selected plaintiffs.

(2) Furthermore, those who fell within the accepted class of close relative who were not present at the scene themselves, but who saw a simultaneous transmission of the accident, satisfied the relevant tests of proximity of time and space to entitle them to recover damages. It was clear from the speeches of the Law Lords in *McLoughlin* that it was not only in relation to the class of people who may come to be able to seek indemnity that the common law must be prepared to move on (by which Hidden J meant expand) but also in the degree of proximity in time and space to the accident, and in relation to the medium by which the shock deriving from the accident is communicated.

Ironically, Hidden J said that the common law is

> entitled to redraw [those lines] where, in the particular case, the court, enlightened by progressive awareness of mental illness, decides.

The irony attaches to the fact that some British (less so American) psychiatrists deny that there is a syndrome, such as post traumatic stress syndrome — by which nervous shock is fashionably becoming known — and insist that there is nothing more than, at best, a cluster of shock related experiences which are, in fact, increasingly poorly understood by lawyers and courts as they move away from the traditional basis for recovery for 'nervous shock'.

(3) As far as the television transmission was concerned, and *mutatis mutandi*, the radio broadcast, it was, according to Hidden J the visual image which was all important:

> the observation through simultaneous television of the scenes of what was happening during the disaster at Hillsborough is sufficient to satisfy the test of proximity of time and space required in such actions as these.

In applying the limiting condition of reasonable foreseeability, Hidden J said that the important question was whether it was

> reasonably foreseeable to the defendant that any negligence of his in respect of persons killed or injured at Hillsborough might lead to psychiatric illness of loved ones of theirs who saw the events live on television? . . . It is accepted that to the defendant it was not merely reasonably foreseeable that the television crews would be [there] . . . but that, in fact of course, he had full knowledge that they would be there. It must be accepted . . . that it was reasonably foreseeable that . . . if unfortunate events took place which changed the event from a joyful sporting occasion to a tragic piece of disastrous news, those cameras would, or might be, used to transmit live pictures.

Comment
This limitation might be used in future to distinguish the broadcast of a news story or other event at which the person responsible for having occasioned the tragedy which is unfolding was unaware as to the presence of television cameras or radio teams; that their presence was not 'reasonably foreseeable'. The importance of the case may be gauged from one example. Following Hidden J's judgment a woman now in her twenties issued proceedings against British Coal (as successors in title to the National Coal Board) claiming damages for the psychiatric harm which she suffered due to the Board's alleged negligent conduct of their operations which occasioned the waste slippage which engulfed her home community of Aberfan in the South Wales valleys in 1966.

Rance v *Mid Downs Health Authority*
The Independent, 13 February 1990

Queen's Bench Division (Brooke J)

Subject matter: Negligence in relation to pre-birth foetal diagnosis — whether actionable in respect of child 'capable of being born alive'.

Plaintiffs claimed that a hospital's medical staff had negligently failed to discover a foetal abnormality and hence deprived the woman of the opportunity of having an abortion. They sought damages for the shock, trauma, distress and pain associated with the subsequent birth and the subsequent cost of bringing up a severely handicapped child. The health authority defended the negligence action by arguing that the scan which would have disclosed the abnormality was carried out at 26 weeks. They argued that the foetus would then have been 'capable of being born alive' and hence that an abortion, even if carried out within the period of 28 weeks, would have been unlawful. They contended that it would be contrary to public policy to award damages for the negligent failure to carry out an unlawful act.

Held

(1) In an extensive review of the formulation and operation of the Infant Life (Preservation) Act 1929, Brooke J found little difficulty with this question of interpretation:

> The difficulty was not with the concept 'capable of being born alive,' but with proving to a jury's satisfaction, without the help of a statutory presumption of information derived from modern technological know-how, that the child in question had those attributes.

He continued that:

> the words 'born alive' are clear, and the meaning of the words 'capable of being born alive' are also clear. . . . [A child is] born alive if, after birth, it exists as a live child, that is to say breathing and living by reason of its breathing through its own lungs alone, without deriving any of its living or power to live by or through

any connection with its mother. . . . Once the foetus has reached a state of development in the womb that it is capable, if born, of possessing those attributes, it is capable of being born within the meaning of the 1929 Act.

Comment
Compare the opinion of the Brightman Committee, the Select Committee of the House of Lords on the Infant Life (Preservation) Bill (1987-8), House of Lords Papers HL50, 1987-88. Brooke J's stress on the child's unaided survival introduces an ambiguity which he had claimed not to discover on the face of s. 1(1) itself. His judgment is open to two interpretations:

(a) that to be capable of being born alive a child must be capable of breathing through its own lungs alone without assistance; or
(b) alternatively, that the independence which the child must possess is that of its mother and independence of any other assistance, mechanical or otherwise, which may be necessary or available

It is, however, consistent with the dicta of Lord Donaldson in *C v S* [1987] 1 All ER 1230, that the breathing must take place other than by or through connection with its mother. That necessary dependence must have been overcome, whether in fact the umbilical link has been broken or not. It is not necessary that the child be able to sustain its lung function without mechanical ventilation. To require otherwise would mean that all the varied circumstances in which neonates might require ventilation, would be cases of children who were not capable of being born alive and failure to attend to them or render medical assistance would not be culpable.

(2) Brooke J went on to consider the submission of counsel for the plaintiffs that 'capable of being born alive' meant viable in the sense of 'being born alive and surviving into old age in the normal way without intensive care or surgical intervention'. This argument was underlined by arguing that, when the Act was passed in 1929, Parliament can only have had in mind the capacity of a neonate to survive naturally and without artificial ventilation or other

assistance. This approach would have avoided the uncertainties introduced by having to specify for how long the survival must be to count as a capacity to be born alive. But Brooke J rejected that interpretation; it would, he said, entail the view that Parliament intended that the phrase it had adopted in the 1929 Act was for individual juries to give substance to, with the result that some children in the course of being born would be denied protection because their expectation of life was not assured at the moment of birth.

B v Islington Health Authority
The Times, 15 November 1990

Queen's Bench Division (Potts J)

Subject matter: Whether plaintiff can sue for pre-birth injury.

The plaintiff's mother underwent a D & C in 1966. At the time she was pregnant with B, the plaintiff. B was born in 1967. She claimed that the medical staff were negligent in and about the performance of the D & C procedure. As a result she suffered great embarrassment about her appearance and would be unable to conceive. The defendant health authority sought an order to strike out the plaintiff's claim for negligence; they alleged that at the time of the negligent act she was an embryo in her mother's womb and hence had no legal status and thus was owed no legal duty by the defendants. The Congenital Disabilities (Civil Liability) Act 1976 made provision as to such civil liability in the case of children born disabled in consequence of some person's fault, but s. 4(5) made the Act apply only to births occurring after and not before its enactment.

Held

(1) When the defendant authority's staff carried out the D & C they ought reasonably to have foreseen that an embryo then in being carried by the mother in her womb was liable to be damaged in the procedure with the result that the living child was liable to be born injured. A reasonable medical person would take account of the risk of causing injury to the embryo in the womb and the consequent risk of the child being born injured and with abnormalities. Were it not for the defendant's submission that the

plaintiff had no right to sue, there would have been no question as to their liability.

(2) Potts J held that the fact that the negligent act which caused the injury was not contemporaneous with the injury itself was not a bar to recovery. The actual damage which was suffered by the plaintiff, i.e., being born suffering from physical abnormalities, was 'potential damage which was foreseeable' and was the result of the breach of a 'possible duty' within the parameters suggested by Lord Pearce in *Dorset Yacht Company Ltd* v *Home Office* [1970] AC 1004. The fact that the plaintiff was undefined in law and without status when the train of events which resulted in that damage was set in motion was not relevant. Although at the time of the negligent act there was in law 'no specific person towards whom the duty could be said to exist' (*Grant* v *Australia Knitting Mills* [1936] AC 85), what had been a 'potential' or 'contingent' duty vested on the birth of the live plaintiff suffering from physical abnormalities caused by the earlier negligent act. There was no legal requirement that the plaintiff and defendant possess correlative rights and duties at the time of the wrongful act. If there was neglect in the D & C procedure in breach of proper medical practice, the risk of injury on birth to a child then being carried by the patient mother was reasonably foreseeable.

(3) Having rejected the defendant's arguments on the question of principle, Potts J held that it was not then open to the court to deny the plaintiff her right to sue based on the defendant's alternative submission that an action brought by her would be contrary to public policy. That argument, based on the hoary old 'floodgates' fear, was inadmissible. Although there will not be likely to be many people who will want or be able to avail themselves of this decision, the 1976 Act now making provision for those born and living for 48 hours (s. 4(4)) after its coming into force, this is a welcome comment on the state of the common law. It may assist those who, like the plaintiff, were injured before the Act came into effect and who have already issued proceedings in time.

(4) Defendant's counsel raised in argument one other possibility which needs consideration. The 1976 Act makes the action available to the child contingent upon injury to the mother or father, and specifically excludes a cause of action against the mother unless it alleges negligence while driving a motor vehicle. Potts J specifically rejected the argument that reasons of public policy

should prevail against recognising the cause of action. In particular, he held that recognition that a common law action could expose a wide range of potential defendants to liability was irrelevant. One such category, counsel had submitted, were parents themselves. A child born with injuries caused by excessive smoking or drinking by the pregnant woman, its mother, might be able to claim against its mother at common law. Time would only begin to run against the child from the age of 18, when the family relationship had deteriorated or broken down and the action was being used in a punitive way. Potts J's rejection of the public policy arguments of the defendants meant that this spectre was floated to be considered again in another case.

F v *Wirral Metropolitan Borough Council*
The Times, 28 May 1990

Court of Appeal (Purchas, Ralph Gibson and Stuart-Smith LJJ)

Subject matter: Liability for interference with parental rights.

The court was confronted with a claim from parents of two children born with phenylketonuria, a metabolic disease calling for skilled dietary management. The local authority social services department formed the view that the parents could not properly provide for the children and they were put into voluntary care. Later the authority assumed rights of parental control over the children. A lengthy series of negotiations between the parents and the authority ensued, in parallel with Mrs F's continued admission and discharge from hospital suffering from depression. When negotiations over a formal resolution of the question of access had finally broken down, the parents issued a writ claiming negligence and/or breach of duty by the defendant's servants or agents causing nervous shock.

Held
The Court of Appeal held that there is no liaiblity for interference with parental rights by a local authority. In a wide ranging judgment which reviewed parents' rights to enjoy consortium with their children, and the effect of the common law and the European Convention on Human Rights in this regard, Purchas LJ questioned the existence of a mutual right of parent and child to enjoy one another's company as part of the fundamental elements of family

life as interpreted in European Court decisions. He concluded that neither under common law nor more recent authority was there such a right in a parent which would found an action for damages. Any parental rights which existed did so for the benefit and protection of the welfare of the child, and not the parent.

Jones v *Northampton Borough Council*
The Independent, 26 May 1990

Court of Appeal (Purchas, Ralph Gibson and Farquharson LJJ)

Subject matter: Duty to warn of apparent danger.

In this case, the litigious hazards of five a side football surfaced when the Court of Appeal considered a question which arose in respect of a duty to warn of an apparent danger. J was injured in a collision with another player following a slip in a pool of rainwater which had leaked through the roof of a sports centre owned by the defendants. The chairman of the sports club for which H was playing had been told that the floor was wet, but had decided to go ahead with the tournament nonetheless. Damages for J's injuries were agreed at £3,000 and the council settled for that amount. It then sought a full contribution from the club chairman under the Civil Liability (Contribution) Act 1978. The question arose, did the chairman owe a duty to J which had been breached?

Held
Ralph Gibson LJ held that he did. The mere fact of a common membership of a club did not by itself give rise to liability, even where as here, one of the members was a member of the committee. However, where a club officer or committee member learned of circumstances giving rise to risk of injury to club members acting as he knew they would if not alerted to the danger, then it was open to the court to find that he owed them a duty of care. Where, as here, the committee member had given no warning of the danger, he or she was in breach of that duty.

Kirkham v *Chief Constable of the Greater Manchester Police*
[1990] 3 All ER 246

Court of Appeal (Lloyd and Farquharson LJJ and Sir Denys Buckley)

Subject matter: *Volenti non fit injuria* and *ex turpi causa non oritur actio*.

This was the first of two cases in which the defence of *ex turpi causa non oritur actio* has been pressed into action. The plaintiff was the widow of a man who had committed suicide in a remand centre. The police had known of his clinical depression which affected his judgment but had failed to tell the staff of the remand centre and the widow sued the police in negligence.

Held
(1) The Court of Appeal held that the defence of *ex turpi* is not limited to cases of criminal conduct but extended to cover any case in which it would affront the public conscience for a damages award to be made. However, they held that the defences of *ex turpi* and *volenti non fit injuria* were not here available to the police. In respect of *ex turpi*, they held that the change in public attitude to suicide did not automatically bar a claim on the basis of the rule and secondly, that the evidence tended to show that the public conscience was not affronted by allowing an award as to damages claimed by the estate of a suicide or following an attempted suicide. Lloyd LJ suggested that where a man of sound mind commits suicide his estate will not be able to maintain an action against the hospital or prison authorities if he is in their care because the maxim *volenti non fit injuria* will provide them with a complete defence.

(2) However, Farquharson LJ doubted that the defence of *volenti non fit injuria* would be appropriate where the act of the deceased relied on to support the defence is the very act which the duty cast upon the defendant required him to prevent; where the deceased is known, or should have been known, to be gravely mentally unstable, then the *volenti* defence will not be available. Although Farquharson LJ joined in saying that the defence of *ex turpi* was not available, he did say that the case might be different, even though suicide or attempted suicide were no longer criminal

offences, where the act was committed by someone who is 'wholly sane'.

Pitts v *Hunt*
[1990] 3 All ER 344

Court of Appeal (Dillon, Balcombe and Beldam LJJ)

Subject matter: *Ex turpi causa non oritur actio*.

The Court had a further opportunity to consider the operation of the defence; this it did extensively. P was a pillion passenger on a motor cycle being driven by the deceased. Both had been to a disco and appeared to have had too much to drink. The motor bike was being ridden at an excessive speed, and appeared to witnesses to be being ridden in a reckless way. In a collision with the second defendant's car P was left permanently disabled. The judge had dismissed his claim for damages on the ground of *ex turpi*.

Held
(1) On appeal Beldam LJ endorsed the views expressed in *Thackwell* v *Barclays Bank* [1986] 1 All ER 676 at 687 and *Saunders* v *Edwards* [1987] 1 WLR 1116 that the court should adopt a pragmatic approach to the defence of *ex turpi*. The court should look at the quality of the illegality and all the surrounding circumstances. The task was to discover:

(a) whether there was an illegality of which the court should take notice; and
(b) to consider whether it would be an affront to the public conscience to compensate the injured party.

Here Beldam LJ argued that although Parliament had provided for the compensation of passengers through compulsory insurance, it had also provided a calendar of criminal offences in order to ensure better road safety. Among those offences, causing death by reckless driving, reckless driving itself and driving while under the influence of drink or drugs were regarded as the most serious. If the offence was so serious that it would preclude the driver from claiming an indemnity under an insurance policy on public policy grounds then public policy would also preclude 'the passenger jointly guilty of that offence from claiming compensation'. The plaintiff here was playing a full and active part in encouraging the deceased to commit serious offences. It would be against public policy to allow recovery of damages, no matter how serious his injuries or his need for compensation. Balcombe and Dillon LJJ delivered concurring judgments which in Dillon LJ's case differed slightly in emphasis.

(2) On two additional important points the Court was clear. The Court held that the effect of the *ex turpi* rule in England and Wales accorded with that in Scotland. Although it was obvious that the plaintiff had voluntarily undertaken to run the risk of injury through his foolhardy actions, s. 148(3) of the Road Traffic Act 1972 (now replaced by Road Traffic Act 1988, s. 149) precluded the ability of a driver to rely on such behaviour as a defence.

(3) Finally, although it was unnecessary to express a concluded view, Beldam LJ said that he differed from the trial judge's opinion that had the defence of *ex turpi* failed, P's damages would in any event have been reduced to nil by virtue of his contributory negligence. On the interpretation of the Law Reform (Contributory Negligence) Act 1945, s. 1, it was clear that the Act began with the premises that P had been injured as a result partly through his or her own fault and partly through the fault of another. Further provisions of the Act made it clear that it was always to be supposed that P would recover some damages, and that therefore a finding of 100 per cent contributory negligence could not be justified.

Morris v *Murray*
[1990] 3 All ER 801

Court of Appeal (Fox and Stocker LJJ and Sir George Waller)

Subject matter: Negligence — defence of *volenti non fit injuria*.

This appeal gave the Court of Appeal another chance to review the operation of the *volenti* defence. The plaintiff was seriously injured in a flying accident which occurred shortly after take-off in a light aircraft being piloted by a man with whom the plaintiff had been drinking heavily. The deceased pilot was found to have had the equivalent of 17 measures of whisky in his blood stream, and the court found that the plaintiff had no compelling reason to make the flight at all.

Held

(1) Here the Court held that the defence was applicable where the plaintiff was capable of understanding that he was embarking on a pleasure flight in a light aircraft with a pilot whose drunkenness was so extreme and glaring that to embark on the flight with him was like engaging in an intrinsically and obviously dangerous operation. Hence a person who was capable of appreciating the risk that was being taken, had implicitly waived any right to damages. Since the plaintiff, although drunk himself, was aware of the risk which he was taking by flying with a drunken pilot and had thereby knowingly and willingly embarked on a flight with a drunken pilot, his claim for damages of nearly £140,000 which had been awarded at trial against the estate of the deceased would be reversed. Fox LJ indicated that it was important in this case to note that the plaintiff had

(a) voluntarily decided to engage in something which was
(b) itself necessarily dangerous.

(2) In cases of negligence *simpliciter*, or where the engagement of the plaintiff had been either required or in which he or she was left with no realistic choice, then the defence of *volenti* might not have been applicable. For instance, suppose that the pilot had been sober at the outset of the flight but had in the course of it consumed vast quantities of alcohol as a result of which the flight became hazardous, then the plaintiff would not have been defeated by the defence of *volenti*. As Fox LJ put it:

> In general, I think that the *volenti* doctrine can apply to the tort of negligence, though it must depend on the extent of the risk, the passenger's knowledge of it and what can be inferred as to his acceptance of it. The passenger cannot be *volens* (in the absence of some form of express disclaimer) in respect of acts of negligence which he had no reason to anticipate and he must be free from compulsion.

Smith v Ainger
The Times, 5 June 1990

Court of Appeal (Neill, Woolf and Butler-Sloss LJJ)

Subject matter: Liability of keeper of dog known to be aggressive.

On the offensive rather than defensive aspects of liability, the anti-dog brigade has been biting back this year. In addition to a plea for dog-shit to be seen as a form of criminal damage, and hence charged under the more serious provisions of the 1971 Act (see Peter Alldridge, *Incontinent Dogs and the Law* (1990) NLJ 1067) the liability of a keeper of a dog known to be aggressive for personal injuries which are caused by that dog was discussed in this case. Section 2(2) of the Animals Act 1971 once again formed the basis of the Court of Appeal's workload (the section has been considered on two previous occasions by an appellate court). This case involved consideration of the result of P's dog lunging at D's dog. In seeking to retain control of his dog, P was pulled off balance, fell into the road and sustained a fracture of his left leg. On the interpretation of s. 2(2) three questions arose:

(a) What did the words 'was likely' in the section mean? ('Where damage is caused by an animal which does not belong to a dangerous species, a keeper of an animal is liable for the damage . . . if . . . the damage is of a kind which the animal, unless restrained, was likely to cause or which, if caused, was likely to be severe . . .').

(b) Was personal injury to a human being the kind of damage which D's dog was likely to cause unless restrained?

(c) Was personal injury, if caused, likely to be severe?

Held

(1) Neill LJ said that on the first question, a broad interpretation should be given. Parliament should not be taken to have intended that a keeper of a dog with a known propensity to bite strangers could escape liability by showing that the dog had bitten only 40 per cent of strangers in the past. 'Was likely' meant 'such as might happen' and not 'probable' or 'more probable than not.'

(2) On the second point, the court decided that the kind of injury in question was personal injury caused by the direct application of force from the animal. It did not, therefore, matter that this force was produced from the consequences of P being buffeted by the dog rather than bitten by it. The injuries suffered constituted damage of the kind which, unless restrained, the dog was likely to cause.

(3) Finally, the court was bound by authority that any injury likely to be caused by this dog was likely to be severe, even though the previous injuries actually caused were quite minor. Damages and interest of £7,200 were awarded.

Eastman v *South West Thames Health Authority*
The Times, 8 May 1990

High Court (Judge J)

Subject matter: Passenger not wearing a seat belt at the time of accident.

This case involved an attempt to reduce the damages liability to a passenger in an ambulance who had not been wearing a seat belt at the time of an accident which caused her injuries. Mrs Eastman sustained serious injuries while accompanying a relative to hospital. The ambulance in which she was travelling braked suddenly, and she was thrown out of her seat. Following *Froome* v *Butcher* [1976] QB 286, it was clear that an adult passenger of reasonable intelligence did not need instruction or warning from the driver in order to wear a seat belt. Such a passenger should know for themselves and could not shift the blame to the driver.

Held
The attempt to avoid liability was defeated. Here the passenger was unfamiliar with the layout of the vehicle; was concerned and anxious about her relative; had been allowed to sit where she chose in the back of the ambulance; had failed to see a notice requesting passengers to wear seat belts and indeed observed the attendant sitting next to the driver not wearing a belt. In the circumstances, Judge J held that the defendant was under a more onerous duty to take reasonable care which required that the attendant indicate in some way that Mrs Eastman should have been using a seat belt or have brought her attention to the notices advising passengers of the advisability of wearing a belt. Had P been given a warning and ignored it, her claim would have failed in part. In the event it succeeded in full.

Porter v Barking and Dagenham LBC
The Times, 4 April 1990

High Court (Simon Brown J)

Subject matter: Duty of care of someone *in loco parentis*.

The caretaker of a comprehensive school had allowed his 14-year-old son and another boy to practise putting the shot after school on school premises using a shot from the school games cupboard. The caretaker did not have the authority to allow any such activities. During the practice P was injured in an accident.

Held

Simon Brown J held that someone standing *in loco parentis* or acting as a parent owed to teenage boys a duty of care to ensure their safety. However the nature of that duty, examined and explained, is not an overbearing one. A balance had to be struck which did not stifle initiative and independence. Teenage boys should not be wholly mollycoddled, and the caretaker's duty was to take care to the standard of the reasonably prudent parent. This ruling will help to define the standard of duty owed by those charged with common law responsibility for the safety of children. As here, much will depend on the age and maturity of the children and the extent to which that is likely to be reflected in their behaviour. Indeed, it may also be that what is known about young boys in general might suggest that where a large group of them gather for a match or an event, then a higher degree of supervision or control might be necessary. On the same argument, the inherent dangerousness of the 'practice' in question will be relevant to the standard of care. Thus boys left unsupervised to practise rugby or fencing or judo might be regarded as unacceptable, whereas with less manifestly hazardous sports a lower degree of supervision and a higher degree of independence would be appropriate.

White v St Albans City and District Council
The Times, 12 March 1990

Court of Appeal (Neill, Nicholls and Bingham LJJ)

Subject matter: The duty owed to trespassers under the Occupier's Liability Act 1984.

CASES

Section 1(3) imposes upon an occupier a duty of care to trespassers if he or she knows or has reasonable grounds to believe that the trespasser may come into the vicinity of the danger. The nature of the duty, imposed by s. 1(4), is to take such care as is reasonable in all the circumstances to see that the trespasser does not suffer injury on the premises by reason of the danger. P was taking a short cut to a car park across fenced-off council owned property when he fell into a 12 ft-deep trench. He unsuccessfully sued for damages for personal injury. On appeal, he contended that once it was established that the occupier had taken precautions (the fencing-off of the land), it followed that the precaution-taker had reason to believe that someone was likely to come into the vicinity of the danger as required by s. 1(3)(b).

Held
Neill LJ rejected that submission. He held that the question to be answered under s. 1(3)(b) could not be answered by appeal to s. 1(4). Rather, the court had to look at the actual state of affairs on the ground when the injury was met with and ask: had the occupier reasonable grounds for believing that someone would come into the vicinity of the danger? Where the accident occurred on private land surrounded with a fence, it was wholly appropriate for the judge to conclude that the council had no reason to believe that anybody in the appellant's position would be in the vicinity of the trench, and hence the trigger for the duty of care was not fired. Despite the fact that Nicholls LJ observed that the fence was insufficient to stop all but the elderly or disabled from entering the land, he agreed with Neill LJ that the consideration of whether an occupier believed that a person was likely to come into vicinity of a danger on land included factors such as fencing and whether there was evidence that the land was used as a short cut to the car park. In this case, there was no such evidence and the appeal failed.

Comment
This decision makes it clear that the statutory protection given to the trespasser by the 1984 Act, following the case of *Herrington* v *British Railways Board* [1972] AC 877, is more illusory than real. It will always be reasonably straightforward for an occupier to show that the conditions for the protection of the trespasser have been satisfied.

Whitfield v *H & R Johnson (Tiles) Ltd*
[1990] 3 All ER 426

Court of Appeal (Purchas and Beldam LJJ and Sir Roger Ormrod)

Subject matter: Liability in respect of accidents at work — employee with congenital back condition which was unknown to the employer.

An important question of liability in respect of accidents at work was raised in this case. P was employed in sorting and packing tiles in D's factory. Aged 36, she suffered from a congenital weakness of the spine. This was unknown to and unsuspected by D. While unloading a tile on to a conveyor belt, P suffered a back injury. She sued her employers for breach of statutory duty, in particular s. 72 of the Factories Act 1961 (as amended). Briefly, the section provides that no person shall be employed to 'lift, carry or move any load so heavy as to be likely to cause injury to him.' Could an employee who was prone to injury rely on this provision in suing the employer?

Held
The Court of Appeal held that P could not. Doubting observations made by the Court in *Bailey* v *Rolls Royce (1971) Ltd* [1984] ICR 688, Beldam LJ held that the likelihood of the injury was to be assessed with regard to whether the weight of the load was appropriate to the gender, build, physique or other obvious physical characteristic (such as relevant disability) of the employee in question, and not to any individual weakness or predisposition to injury of a particular employee. The likelihood of injury to the employee had to arise from his being employed to lift an object of a weight which in all the circumstances was excessive. Such considerations included the nature of the object, the grip the employee could take of it, the foothold available, and all the other relevant circumstances, but not those particular to the employee.

De Souza v *Home and Overseas Insurance Co Ltd*
The Times, 19 September 1990

Court of Appeal (Mustill, Nourse and Butler-Sloss LJJ)

Subject matter: Nature of 'accidental bodily injury'.

CASES

In this case the Court was asked to consider whether 'heatstroke' was an accidental bodily injury. P was the widow of a man who had died of heatstroke while on holiday in Torremolinos, Spain. His widow sought recovery under an insurance policy which provided for payment where the insured had suffered 'accidental bodily injury caused solely and directly by violent and visible means . . .' The trial judge had felt constrained by authority to hold that this included heatstroke. On appeal, Mustill LJ said that the authorities on workmen's compensation were of limited value and that the more straightforward insurance cases provided a firmer line of authority. The phrase 'outward violent and visible means' related not to a condition precedent to liability but served to expound the expression 'accidental bodily injury'.

Held
An accident was not established merely by showing that the assured did not foresee the consequences of what he or she chose to do. An ordinary, literate lay person if asked whether the deceased had been the victim of accidental injury would have replied 'of course not'. The judge's first instinct, unfettered by authority, had been to agree with that assessment. His instinct and not the authorities had been correct; the appeal was allowed.

Hughes v *Waltham Forest Health Authority*
The Times, 9 November 1990

Court of Appeal (Fox, Butler-Sloss and Beldam LJJ)

Subject matter: Medical negligence.

The plaintiff had been awarded £220,000 damages for breach of duty of care in an operation performed by two surgeons employed by the defendants. At the trial, two other distinguished surgeons had been called to give evidence on behalf of the plaintiff. They considered that the defendant's surgeons had fallen below the duty of care to be expected of competent surgeons.

Held
Allowing the defendants' appeal, it was not sufficient, to establish that the defendants had been negligent, simply to produce expert evidence which demonstrated that two other surgeons would not

have proceeded in the manner adopted by the defendants. Indeed, it did not prove that the defendants had fallen short of the standard of care to be expected of them to show that the decision ultimately turned out to be mistaken. Beldam LJ said that the question which the judge should have asked, applying *Maynard* v *West Midlands Regional Health Authority* [1984] 1 WLR 634, was whether the surgeons in reaching their decision displayed such a lack of clinical judgment that no surgeon exercising proper care and skill could have reached the same decision. If the judge had applied that test, he could only have arrived at the conclusion that fault had not been proved against the defendants.

Damages

A guide to the quantum of damages cases reported in 1990 is given on p.71.

Pidduck v *Eastern Scottish Omnibuses*
[1990] 2 All ER 69

Court of Appeal (Purchas and Glidewell LJJ and Sir Roger Ormrod)

Subject matter: Fatal Accidents Act 1976 — 'benefits'.

P had lost her only income — her husband's pension — when he was killed in an accident for which D admitted liability.

Held

The Court of Appeal held that payments to a widow from a pension fund directly consequent upon her husband's death are 'benefits' to be disregarded under s. 4 of the Fatal Accidents Act 1976 when awarding damages. Because the pension scheme had provided the deceased but not P with a pension, the money which became payable on his death were 'benefits which had accrued as a result of the deceased's death' within s. 4 and hence not merely benefits which had accrued as a result of her husband's death. P was entitled to a sum for loss of dependency until trial irrespective of the receipts from the pension fund.

Wood v *British Coal Corporation*
The Times, 10 October 1990

Court of Appeal (Parker, Stuart-Smith and Leggatt LJJ)

Subject matter: Credit against a claim for loss of earnings of monies from a pension scheme — application of *Parry* v *Cleaver* [1970] AC 1.

The appellant had been a mineworker who had retired due to incapacity following an accident at work. In his action for personal injuries against the BCC, the judge had in arriving at his calculation for loss of earnings, deducted payments to which the plaintiff was entitled under the mineworkers' pension scheme to which his employers — the tortfeasor — had contributed. The case turned on first, whether there was any material distinction between this case and that of *Parry* v *Cleaver* [1970] AC 1, and secondly, if the case could be distinguished, whether the principles of common law that the plaintiff should recover no more than he has lost were applicable to ensure that there was no 'double recovery'. The judge had held that the difference was material and had ordered a deduction. On appeal:

Held

(1) That a plaintiff who sustained an injury at work and had to retire because he was incapacitated did not have to give credit against a claim for loss of earnings of monies which he had received from such a pension scheme. The defendant had argued that *Parry* could be distinguished because in this case BCC — the tortfeasor — made contributions to the pension scheme, whereas in *Parry* the tortfeasor had not been the plaintiff's employer and was a third party unconnected with the plaintiff's pension scheme. Stuart-Smith LJ, giving the leading judgment, held that when *Parry* was decided, exceptions to the principle disallowing double recovery were based on justice, reasonableness and public policy, and that two were well recognised and endorsed by the majority in *Parry*;

    (a)   that the proceeds of private insurance taken out by the plaintiff should not be deducted from an award of damages,
    (b)   that charitable and benevolent receipts from third parties were similarly exempt.

It was fundamental to the notion that justice and reason did not require deduction of the pension that the pension had been bought by the fruit of the plaintiff's own past labour. It was this approach which made it impossible for the defendant to contend that justice and reason demanded in the present case that the pension should be deducted on the ground that the defendant tortfeasor had contributed to the pension fund. The defendant was bound as a matter of contract to make those payments to the plaintiff; it was a benefit to the plaintiff and was part of the consideration for the work which the plaintiff was required to do. It was not something which the defendant did gratuitously or as a matter of benevolence. In the absence of an express or implied contractual term that payment of pension should be deducted from any damages awarded against the defendant, there was no material difference between this case and *Parry*, and the fact that the defendant contributed to the pension scheme did not make that difference.

(2) On the defendant's submission that the pension receipts were not distinguishable from unemployment benefit, which fell to be deducted from loss of earnings in calculating a plaintiff's damages, Stuart-Smith LJ held that there was a clear distinction between unemployment benefit on the one hand and benefits under a personal insurance policy or pension on the other, as had been recognised by Sellers LJ in *Parsons* v *B N M Laboratories* [1964] 1 QB 95.

Corbett v *Barking, Havering and Brentwood Health Authority*
The Times, 24 May 1990

Court of Appeal (Purchas, Gibson and Farquharson LJJ)

Subject matter: Damages — effect of delay on multiplier.

The plaintiff's mother had died during childbirth in 1977. The claim was not brought for a long period of time, such that at trial there was only six months of the assessed dependency left to run. In assessing damages under the Fatal Accidents Act 1976 payable to the 11½-year-old, the judge took no account of the pre-trial delay or of the known fact of the dependant's survival before the case came on. The court reduced the multiplier of 18 using the normal discounts to produce a multiplier of 12 from the date of death. He awarded a multiplicand of £2,600 per annum for future care. Damages were awarded under this head of only £1,300, based on an unexpired multiplier of six months.

Held

(1) (Ralph Gibson LJ dissenting) On appeal a majority of the Court of Appeal held that the multiplier should have been adjusted in order to take account of the removal of many of the uncertainties surrounding the provision and receipt of the dependency during the relevant period. The issue at the heart of the appeal was the date at which the known facts should have been taken account of in making the various calculations which the court was required to make.

The usual discount from the 18-year period of dependency should be reduced accordingly. However, the use of the multiplier approach for the capitalisation of future damages to be compensated by a once-and-for-all lump sum, while an adequate and well-known instrument had, according to Purchas LJ, to be used appropriately. In every assessment for future damages to be compensated by an immediate payment there were at least five essential elements:

(a) the likelihood of the provider of the support continuing to exist;
(b) the likelihood of the dependant being alive to benefit from that support;
(c) the possibility of the providing capacity of the provider being affected by the changes and chances of life either in a positive or a negative manner;
(d) the possibility of the needs of the dependant being altered by those same chances and changes, and again either in a positive or a negative way;
(e) an actuarial discount to compensate:

(i) for immediate receipt of compensatory damages in advance of the date when the loss would have in fact occurred;
(ii) for the fact that the capital should be exhausted at the end of the period of dependency.

(2) Purchas LJ said that as a general rule, to arrive at a multiplier, it was necessary to consider the combined effect of (a)

and (c) to arrive at the number of years during which provision of support was likely to be available if needed; to consider the combined effect of (b) and (d) together to arrive at the number of years during which support was likely to be needed by the dependant; to apply (e) to the lesser of the two calculations with an additional but usually minor discount to take account of the outside chance that the choice between the two sums might be wrong. There was no authority (such as *Graham* v *Dodds* [1983] 1 WLR 808 (HL)) which required, as the judge had wrongly believed, the court to disregard facts established at trial, such that the multiplier to be assessed as at the date of death could not be adjusted. (On this point Ralph Gibson LJ dissented, believing that the court was prevented by *Graham* v *Dodds* from adjusting the multiplier to take into account the facts arising from the delay before the trial took place.)

(3) Using its substituted discretion for that of the judge, Purchas and Farquharson LJJ said that they would set a multiplier of 15 from which 11½ should be deducted for the pre-trial delay period. The majority would award a figure of £9,100 under this head.

Stanley v *Saddique*
The Times, 24 May 1990

Court of Appeal (Purchas and Ralph Gibson LJJ and Sir David Croom-Johnson)

Subject matter: Fatal Accidents Act 1976, s. 4, as amended — Administration of Justice Act 1982, s. 3 — benefits to be disregarded.

The plaintiff's mother left her husband in order to live with another man, by whom she became pregnant with the plaintiff in 1983. At the time of the woman's death (in a road accident caused by the defendant's negligence in March 1984) the father looked after the plaintiff. In June that year the father met another woman, T, whom he married in November 1984. The judge found that after his marriage to T, the plaintiff's father 'settled down' and became a good father to the plaintiff, to T's daughter and to another child who was subsequently born. The judge also found that T provided the plaintiff with 'mothering services' of a higher quality than could foreseeably be expected to have been provided by the minor's mother, which would have been of an indifferent quality, lacking in continuity, and, given that she had already left one handicapped and one extremely young child for an irresponsible relationship, unreliable. He held, however, that the benefits provided by this alternative home were excluded by s. 4 of the 1976 Act from being taken into account in assessing the damages to which the plaintiff was entitled.

Held

(1) The benefit accruing to a minor, whose unreliable mother was killed in a car accident, through his father's marriage to a more reliable woman who provided a higher standard of motherly services, was a benefit which was properly disregarded by the judge under s. 4 in assessing the plaintiff's damages. The benefits not subject to being taken into account were not limited, as the defendant had contended, to direct pecuniary benefits. That interpretation would have robbed the statutory scheme of much of the improvement which it had wrought over the common law rules.

(2) It could not be said that there was no loss of dependency to the minor. However, the deceased mother's shortcomings was a matter which should be taken into account when calculating the damages for loss of dependency. The defendant argued that the judge had not taken into account, when taking a multiplier of 12 to cover the plaintiff's dependency up to the age of 18, the possibility that the mother might, as a result of her own shortcomings, not be available during the full 12-year period. The mother's previous family history and the minor's prospects of having enjoyed any continuing or valuable support from his mother were bleak, they argued. Purchas LJ held that the judge's computation was plainly too high and was reached on a wrong principle, in as much as it omitted to make a proper discount for the real possibility that the mother would not have stayed with the family. Such was the lack of steady prospect of support that the multiplier/multiplicand approach which the judge had adopted, following *Spittle* v *Bunney* [1988] 1 WLR 847, was inappropriate. In carrying out an assessment on a 'jury award basis' Purchas LJ substituted a figure of £10,000 for loss of services, and £5,000 for loss of financial support. The total award on appeal was therefore £15,000, compared with the £34,536 which the judge had awarded using the multiplier/multiplicand method.

Champion v *London Fire and Civil Defence Authority*
The Times, 5 July 1990

Queen's Bench Division (Mr H Carlisle QC, sitting as a deputy judge)

Subject matter: Damages for loss of congenial employment.

The plaintiff had slipped on some broken eggs which had been knocked onto the floor by a fellow fire officer in the kitchen at Surbiton Fire Station. He had fractured his wrist in the fall. His colleague had made a statement accepting responsibility for the accident. As a result of his injury, the plaintiff had to be discharged from the fire service. He sought damages for loss of congenial employment because he had lost his job. The defendants raised two issues; first, that the statement by his colleague was inadmissible for the purposes of showing the negligence of the defendants, and secondly, that damages had already been agreed for general damages for pain and suffering, which should be taken to include a sum in respect of the loss of particular enjoyment derived from the employment.

Held

(1) That the colleague's statement was not admissible in evidence against his employers as the colleague could not be treated as an agent of the Authority. For it to be admissible, it would have to be shown to be made with the authority of the defendants, or to have been made to a third party and not to one of the principals in the case. Admissions by employees were not usually admissible where the plaintiff was suing a fellow employee. However, the judge said that the statement would be admitted under the provisions of RSC Ord. 38 r. 29(2), which gives the court a discretion to admit a statement to be given in evidence at trial or hearing if a refusal to exercise that power might oblige the party desiring to give the statement in evidence to call as a witness at trial or hearing an opposite party or person who is or was at the material time the servant or agent of an opposite party.

(2) The court accepted that the plaintiff had suffered a significant loss of job satisfaction, and that damages would normally have been awarded under the head of general damages for pain and suffering. But where damages under that head had already been

agreed between the parties, excluding the element of loss of congenial employment, the court would make a separate award for loss of job satisfaction.

Middleton v *Elliott Turbo Machinery*
The Times, 29 October 1990

Court of Appeal (Mustill, Butler-Sloss and Beldam LJJ)

Subject matter: Provisional damages award coupled with a declaration.

The plaintiff was a former shipyard worker who, in 1980 and 1985, had suffered illnesses which were reflections of a benign asbestos-related pleurisy attributable to his employment. It was established that at some time in the future there was a small risk that he might develop asbestoses or lung cancer. There was a greater risk, still put at less than 50 per cent, of his suffering illness that would put him permanently out of work. The plaintiff was awarded immediate provisional damages of £10,000 under RSC Ord. 37 r. 10 and a declaration that if he suffered any of those conditions he would be entitled to make application for further damages. The judge also made a declaration in the following terms:

> that as much of the judgment as gives the plaintiff conditional right to apply for further damages at a future date is not, and, unless and until further damages be awarded, will not be such judgment or satisfaction as precludes a claim by his surviving dependants upon the Fatal Accidents Act 1976 for damages corresponding with the said further damages.

The defendants appealed against this declaration.

Held
A declaration attached to a judgment awarding a plaintiff provisional damages that his dependants be entitled, in the event of his death from such disease, to recover further damages under the Fatal Accidents Act 1976 was not lawful. Mustill LJ said that the plaintiff had had a choice; to an immediate award in relation to the risk that serious consequences would ensue or to an immediate award of provisional damages, with a right to return later should he

become ill. He had chosen the latter route. However, he sought to have his interests in his family's well-being protected by safeguarding them against the possibility of receiving nothing as a consequence of his having made the wrong choice. He advanced two arguments which had persuaded the judge to declare the law in a sense favourable to the plaintiff;

(a) that there was an existing issue between him and the defendants in relation to which he had important interests which ought to be safeguarded;

(b) there were many instances of plaintiffs in a similar position who wished to know the consequences of having obtained a provisional award.

The Court of Appeal had no ground upon which it could intervene, said Mustill LJ, when the plaintiff had chosen to take a provisional award rather than pressing for an immediate award of the whole sum. The appellate function could not be discharged by seeking to have the court act as a purveyor of advice through the expression of opinions which were sought as binding precedents. Not only was the event against which protection was sought more likely not to happen than it was to happen; if a claim were to arise, it would not be brought by parties to the present action; persons whose identity could not now be accurately predicted and might not now even be alive. The appeal against that part of the judgment which had contained the declaration was allowed.

Quantum of Damages
Personal Injuries or Death

The table below is a cumulative guide to quantum of damages cases reported in Current Law in 1990 and is reproduced with kind permission of Sweet & Maxwell Ltd.

Injury	Age (at time of injury unless otherwise stated)	Case	Award General	Total	Reference
			£	£	
Death	21	Pyre v Devenport Management	148,000		12 C.L. 180
Quadriplegia	birth	O'Donnell v South Bedfordshire HA	105,000	346,476.25	12 C.L. 180
	24	Bowden v Lane	100,000	949.524.54	12 C.L. 180
Spastic Quadriplegia	6 months	Thompson v South Tees Area Health Authority	100,000	613,734	6 C.L. 210
Multiple Injuries	13	Smith, Re	27,500		12 C.L. 180
	36	Nelson v Page	7,000		2 C.L. 97
	38	Lakhrissi, Re	3,750		8 C.L. 251
Injuries to Brain and Skull	30	Gregory, Re	55,000	137,000	10 C.L. 220
	18	Crompton v Peacock	25,000		11 C.L. 229
	19	Power v Kitchener	16,000		5 C.L. 157
	60	Bellovics v British Railways Board	4,500		11 C.L. 229
	10	Williams, Re	4,500		6 C.L. 210
Epilepsy	21	Adams, Re	50,000	204,304	12 C.L. 180
Face	23	Branch v Lowe	4,000		12 C.L. 180
	33 (at date of trial)	Rowland, Re	1,750	4,500	11 C.L. 229
Face and Ear	59 (at date of hearing)	Jones, Re	2,750		3 C.L. 146
Nose	22	Mitchem v Kefford	4,000		5 C.L. 157
	39	Singh, Re	3,500		3 C.L. 146
Teeth	16	McKenna v Heron	3,000		7 C.L. 192
Scarring	20	Todd, Re	4,500		12 C.L. 180
	16	Litchfield v Flear	4,000		12 C.L. 180
Burns	33 (at date of trial)	Barraclough v B. and H. Pies	1,500		5 C.L. 157
Skin	59 (at date of trial)	Arkley v Alfred Ellis and Sons (Wakefield)	8,000		9 C.L. 199
Sight	unknown	Lindsell, Re	25,000		11 C.L. 229
	29	Lingard v C. U. Stubbs & Sons	20,000		7 C.L. 192

CASES

Injury	Age (at time of injury unless otherwise stated)	Case	Award General £	Total £	Reference
	53	Evans, Re	20,000		4 C.L. 132
	23	Redfern, Re	12,000		11 C.L. 229
	unknown	Forshaw v G.E.C.	8,000		10 C.L. 220
	20	Lynch, Re	6,500		6 C.L. 210
Hearing	30	Okine, Re	30,000		12 C.L. 180
Neck	39	Thomas v Fury	6,500		4 C.L. 132
	33	Chappell v Chief Constable of Hertfordshire	6,000		5 C.L. 157
	39	Corthorn v Foster	5,000		4 C.L. 132
	33	Rowe v Waddringham Technical Services	4,250		4 C.L. 132
	55	Gardner v Mullins	3,750	4,525	11 C.L. 229
	55	Miles v Martyn	3,750		11 C.L. 229
	53	Fulton v Turners (Southampton)	3,500		2 C.L. 97
	45	Crews v Harrison	3,000		11 C.L. 229
Spine	36	Wolf v Anafield Builders	20,000		9 C.L. 199
	45	Vincent, Re	17,500		7 C.L. 192
	17	Pedley v Timmins	14,000		8 C.L. 251
	38	Hinnigan v Jackson	10,000		12 C.L. 180
	27	Owen v Grimsby & Cleethorpes Transport	10,000		1 C.L. 108
	46	Butler v Guildford Borough Council	8,500	50,467	6 C.L. 210
	38	Gee v Bayes	7,500, (12,500 if pre-existing condition not involved)		7 C.L. 192
	unknown	Franks v British Railways Board	7,500		9 C.L. 199
	37	Desborough v Carlisle City Council	6,500	8,587	6 C.L. 210
	55	Saggers v Lea Valley Regional Park Authority	6,500		12 C.L. 180
	49	Fox v London Transport Executive	5,000		2 C.L. 97
	32	Bell v Walsh	1,750		1 C.L. 108
Respiratory Organs	52 (at date of trial)	Kent v Wakefield Metal Traders	45,000	142,634.36	11 C.L. 229
	49 (at date of trial)	Leal v British Sugar	17,500		9 C.L. 199
	50 (at date of trial)	Davies v Newalls Insulation	5,000		10 C.L. 220
Chest	27	Ravenscroft v Clarke	2,000		5 C.L. 157

CASES

Injury	Age (at time of injury unless otherwise stated)	Case	Award General	Total	Reference
			£	£	
Bowel	31	Bovenzi v Kettering Health Authority	6,000		11 C.L. 229
Hip	52	Charalambous v Andreou	16,000		3 C.L. 146
Shoulder	67 (at date of hearing)	Harrow-Bunn, Re	8,000		9 C.L. 199
	79 (at date of trial)	Lennon v McDonald	2,750		3 C.L. 146
Arm	23	Green v Wilson	35,000	169,563.50	12 C.L. 180
	25	Morton v Chief Constable of Cumbria	10,000 (assessed)		2 C.L. 97
	77	Voller v Smith	4,250		8 C.L. 251
	11	Type v Merthyr Tydfil Borough Council	1,600		5 C.L. 157
Wrist	24	Braithwaite v Latham	8,250		6 C.L. 210
	51	Harrison v Pilkington Glass	6,000		9 C.L. 199
	63	Smithies v Eatoughs	5,250		11 C.L. 229
Hand	47	Antony, Re	45,000		8 CL 251
	30	O'Brien v Berol	6,500		1 C.L. 108
	48	Peters v Worthing District Health Authority	2,500	2,990	11 C.L. 229
Fingers	25 (at date of trial)	Steventon v Cotmor Tool and Presswork Co.	40,000	113,250	4 C.L. 132
	48 (at date of trial)	Daniel v Valor Heating	20,000	34,803	3 C.L. 146
	40	Thomas v Howmet Turbine (U.K.) Inc.	7,000		8 C.L. 251
	22	Streatfield v Long	4,500		6 C.L. 210
	20s	Taylor v I.M.I. Yorkshire Imperial	3,000		9 C.L. 199
	49 (at date of trial)	Rosamond v TRW Valves	2,750		10 C.L. 220
	54	Waudby v Humberside County Council	2,000		1 C.L. 108
Thumb	48	Butterfield v Clifford Williams & Son	650		1 C.L. 108
Knee	23	Henderson v Watchorn	12,000		7 C.L. 192
	31 (at date of trial)	Smith v Jager	8,500		4 C.L. 132
	32	Stannard v Durham County Council	5,000		12 C.L. 180

Injury	Age (at time of injury unless otherwise stated)	Case	Award General	Total	Reference
			£	£	
Chest	27	Ravenscroft v Clarke	2,000		5 C.L. 157
Bowel	31	Bovenzi v Kettering Health Authority	6,000		11 C.L. 229
Hip	52	Charalambous v Andreou	16,000		3 C.L. 146
Shoulder	67 (at date of hearing)	Harrow-Bunn, Re	8,000		9 C.L. 199
	79 (at date of trial)	Lennon v McDonald	2,750		3 C.L. 146
Arm	23	Green v Wilson	35,000	169,563.50	12 C.L. 180
	25	Morton v Chief Constable of Cumbria	10,000 (assessed)		2 C.L. 97
	77	Voller v Smith	4,250		8 C.L. 251
	11	Type v Merthyr Tydfil Borough Council	1,600		5 C.L. 157
Wrist	24	Braithwaite v Latham	8,250		6 C.L. 210
	51	Harrison v Pilkington Glass	6,000		9 C.L. 199
	63	Smithies v Eatoughs	5,250		11 C.L. 229
Hand	47	Antony, Re	45,000		8 CL 251
	30	O'Brien v Berol	6,500		1 C.L. 108
	48	Peters v Worthing District Health Authority	2,500	2,990	11 C.L. 229
Fingers	25 (at date of trial)	Steventon v Cotmor Tool and Presswork Co.	40,000	113,250	4 C.L. 132
	48 (at date of trial)	Daniel v Valor Heating	20,000	34,803	3 C.L. 146
	40	Thomas v Howmet Turbine (U.K.) Inc.	7,000		8 C.L. 251
	22	Streatfield v Long	4,500		6 C.L. 210
	20s	Taylor v I.M.I. Yorkshire Imperial	3,000		9 C.L. 199
	49 (at date of trial)	Rosamond v TRW Valves	2,750		10 C.L. 220
	54	Waudby v Humberside County Council	2,000		1 C.L. 108
Thumb	48	Butterfield v Clifford Williams & Son	650		1 C.L. 108
Knee	23	Henderson v Watchorn	12,000		7 C.L. 192
	31 (at date of trial)	Smith v Jager	8,500		4 C.L. 132
	32	Stannard v Durham County Council	5,000		12 C.L. 180

CASES

Injury	Age (at time of injury unless otherwise stated)	Case	Award General	Total	Reference
			£	£	
	37	Burton v Frigoscandia	2,250		11 C.L. 229
Knee and Legs	23	Hardy v Doldorph	17,500		3 C.L. 146
Leg above knee	19	Norton v Rentokil	22,500		8 C.L. 251
	25 (at date of hearing)	Newton, Re	9,000		9 C.L. 199
	2¾	Francis v Neal	4,000		7 C.L. 192
Leg below knee	21	McGuirk v Hardie & Atkinson	5,000		5 C.L. 157
	78	Nelson v Nelson Taxis (Teesside)	2,200		10 C.L. 220
Leg and Ankle	37 (at date of trial)	Jones v Houlder Marine Drilling	16,500		9 C.L. 199
Ankle	17	Everard v Unigate Dairies	18,000		10 C.L. 220
	55	Johnson v Rolls Royce	4,250		10 C.L. 220
Asthma	(birth through childhood)	Bygraves v London Borough of Southwark	7,000		10 C.L. 220
Psychological	25 (at date of trial)	Steventon v Cotmor Tool and Presswork Co.	40,000	113,250	4 C.L. 132
	13	R, Re	20,000		8 C.L. 251
	5	T, Re	20,000		7 C.L. 192
	3	G, Re	20,000		7 C.L. 192
	9 (at date of hearing)	E, Re	17,500		5 C.L. 157
	19 (at date of hearing)	J, Re	17,500		9 C.L. 199
	11 (at date of hearing)	J, Re	15,000		5 C.L. 157
	7 (at date of hearing)	K, Re	12,500		5 C.L. 157
	5 (at date of hearing)	D, Re	12,500		5 C.L. 157
	17 (at date of hearing)	N, Re	12,500		9 C.L. 199
	30	H, Re	10,000		12 C.L. 180
	35	Simpson, Re	10,000		9 C.L. 199
	22	X, Re	10,000		3 C.L. 140
	15 (at date of hearing)	P, Re	7,500		1 C.L. 108
	45	Inkersole, Re	7,000		6 C.L. 210
	31	Claringbold, Re	5,000		11 C.L. 229
	2	J, Re	5,000		7 C.L. 192
	16	S, Re	3,500	5,750	12 C.L. 180
	9	Hunt v Clancy	2,500		10 C.L. 220

Injury	Age (at time of injury unless otherwise stated)	Case	Award General	Total	Reference
			£	£	
	3	Misiri v Milner	2,500		10 C.L. 220
	26	Cunningham, Re	1,500		6 C.L. 210
Haematoma	41	Speechly v Spencer	3,000		10 C.L. 220
Minor Injuries	51	Farrell v Porn and Dunwoody	2,000		7 C.L. 192
	4	Hopgood v Homebase	2,000		12 C.L. 180
	29	Doden v Lowings	1,800		9 C.L. 199
	55	Frazer v Courtaulds	1,750		12 C.L. 180
	29	Arrighi v Brewers	1,650		12 C.L. 180
	32	Japal v Ford Motor Co.	1,600		4 C.L. 132
	29	Thomas v London Regional Transport	1,250		4 C.L. 132
	60	Bedford Valene v Hopkins & Shaw T/A Access Central	1,200		7 C.L. 192
	unknown	Dolton v Studley	1,150		8 C.L. 251
	17	Ralph v Smith	1,100		7 C.L. 192
	63 (at date of trial)	Littleford v Wood	1,000		2 C.L. 97
	23	Horesh v Ryman	1,000		8 C.L. 251
	50 (at date of trial)	Heskey v G.K.N. Sankey	1,000		10 C.L. 220
	49	Hanks v Courtaulds	750		8 C.L. 251
	57	Hill, Re	750		12 C.L. 180
	24	Rice v Garrett	750		8 C.L. 251
	unknown	Larcombe v Willis	750		8 C.L. 251
	7, 5	March v The Post Office	750 (each)		11 C.L. 229
	41	Baughan v Paxton	700		11 C.L. 229
	28	Brown v Hillier	700		12 C.L. 180
	38	Moon v Lake	700		6 C.L. 210
	42 (at date of trial)	Walley v Linney	700		5 C.L. 157
	22	Williams v Russell	650		2 C.L. 97
	68	Coombs v Roberts	500	1,661.03	11 C.L. 229
	unknown	O'Hanlon v Merseyside Passenger Transport Executive	500		10 C.L. 220
	37	Munson v Richardson	475		9 C.L. 199
	2 years, 3 months	Babla v Patel	450		4 C.L. 132
	19, 21	Jackson & Jackson v Mourne	400	400	3 C.L. 146
	3½, 2½	Hope v Money	£350 (each)		11 C.L. 229
	unknown	Archer & Archer v Leighton & Marsh	300		7 C.L. 192

CASES

Injury	Age (at time of injury unless otherwise stated)	Case	Award General	Total	Reference
			£	£	
	34	Edwards v Oxytech Services	200		11 C.L. 229
	39, 29	James and Evand v Keenan	200	250	3 C.L. 146
	48	Nicholson v Bolton	200		9 C.L. 199
	50	Wright v Cole	200		6 C.L. 210
	22	Morgan v Inco Alloys	50 (assessed)		6 C.L. 210
		Scottish cases			
Chronic asthma	mid-20's	Reilly v Robert Kellie & Son	12,000		1 C.L. 726
Head	27	Laidler v Yarrow Shipbuilders	2,500	4,500	3 C.L. 754
Brain and Skull	41 (at date of proof)	O'Brien's C.B. v British Steel	60,000		5 C.L. 754
Back	20	Gorman v McLaren	4,000		5 C.L. 753a
Head and Leg	19	Clarke v McFadyen	7,500	11,107	3 C.L. 750
Shoulder	(age not known)	MacFarlane v Greater Glasgow Health Board	4,000		1 C.L. 724
Shoulder (plus depression)	43	McCrae v Durastic	12,500	86,325	1 C.L. 725
Arm	36	Weldon v British Coal Corporation	3,000		1 C.L. 799
Knee	47	Gow v Dundee Stevedores	13,500		2 C.L. 742
	27	Aitken v Midlothian District Council		8,500	1 C.L. 722
Thumb	34	Allan v British Coal Corporation	400		1 C.L. 723
Death		Davidson v Upper Clyde Shipbuilders	Loss of society	9,500 (widow)	3 C.L. 752

Practice and procedure

Re HIV Haemophiliac Litigation
The Independent, 2 October 1990

Court of Appeal (Ralph Gibson and Bingham LJJ and Sir John Megaw)

Subject matter: Claims for compensation and public interest immunity.

In this important case concerning the infection of nearly 1,000 haemophiliacs with the HIV virus, the Court of Appeal was asked to order disclosure of documents for which public interest immunity had been claimed.

Held

Limited disclosure was allowed. Where a prima facie case of negligence is established, the public interest in a full and fair trial of the plaintiff's claims overrides a government department's claim to public interest immunity.

Comment

While Ralph Gibson LJ acknowledged that it was difficult to prove a negligent breach of duty when the Department of Health and other health authorities against whom the allegation was made were required to exercise discretion and form judgments on the allocation of public resources, that was not sufficient to make it clear that there could be no claim against them. Bingham LJ said that the balancing exercise between the public interest immunity and the public interest in a fair trial of the claim made by a large body of grievously injured plaintiffs, and the public recognition that the claim had been fully and openly tried, came down decisively in favour of the plaintiffs.

Singh v *London Underground*
The Independent, 25 April 1990

Queen's Bench Division (Mr John Peppitt QC sitting as a deputy judge)

Subject matter: Jury trials in personal injury claims.

The use of jury trials in personal injury actions is very rare indeed these days. However, following the King's Cross underground fire in which 31 people died, P sought the installation of a jury to hear a claim for damages for injuries suffered after the fire. P's son, daughter and grandson had been killed in the fire, and he was claiming for continued psychiatric illness, which has become known as post traumatic stress disorder. The same question arose in the judgment of Hidden J in the case involving claims arising from the Hillsborough Stadium deaths. In this case, however, P additionally sought exemplary and aggravated damages under the heads established in *Rookes* v *Barnard* [1964] AC 1129. In this he argued that a jury trial was appropriate where the findings of fact and the determination of corporate liability were likely to be of general public concern.

Held
(1) The judge said that a discretionary order for jury trials should not be made under s. 69(3) of the Supreme Court Act 1981 unless there were exceptional circumstances. Here, there were exceptional features, in that the claim concerned the conduct of a public corporation responsible for the safety of London's travelling public and raised questions about that conduct which went far beyond the plaintiff's own claim.
(2) However, the defence's argument was that the case would involve witnesses going into technical matters and the production of a large number of documents, many of which would be complex. An investigation to deal with the claims for aggravated and exemplary damages would entail examining such wide issues as the financial structure of London Underground; the philosophy of the operation, safety procedure, financial structure and policy, and its funding base. A trial with jury was likely, therefore, to prove unmanageable, according to counsel for the defence. With this the judge agreed. It was important to take into account that a judge would have a difficult task marshalling all these documents and arguments. It was not advisable that he or she should be burdened with a jury as well.
(3) In addition, it was appropriate to take into account subsidiary matters such as the increase in the length of the trial that a jury would entail, as well as the logistics of finding court space. On balance, the investigation called for by the plaintiff's claim for exemplary and aggravated damages was better dealt with by a judge alone.

Donovan v *Gwentoys Ltd*
[1990] 1 All ER 1018

House of Lords (Lord Bridge of Harwich, Lord Templeman, Lord Griffiths, Lord Oliver of Aylmerton and Lord Lowry)

Subject matter: Limitation Act 1980, s. 33.

In 1979 the plaintiff, then aged 16, slipped while at work. She strained her wrist and aggravated a pre-existing knee complaint. She received industrial injury payments but did not mention the knee injury to her employers. In 1980 she left the defendant's employment, and then shortly before the limitation period ran out she consulted solicitors who applied for legal aid but failed to protect her position by serving a writ. The limitation period ran out three years after the plaintiff's 18th birthday in April 1984. Thereafter a catalogue of partial disclosures in September 1984 (plaintiff's solicitors informed defendants of intention to sue but not of date of accident, nature of injury or alleged negligence), October 1984 (writ issued), January 1985 (statement of claim served revealing that plaintiff was alleging she slipped on plastic bag for the presence of which defendants were being blamed), January 1986 (defendants first informed of the real nature of the claim when medical report disclosed injury to knee) and June 1987 (date of the accident finally disclosed) enabled the defendants to discover that they may have a limitation defence available to them anyway. The defendants applied to have the case struck out as statute barred, and the plaintiff applied for the exercise of the court's discretion under s. 33 of the Limitation Act 1980, to disapply the provisions of s. 11. The defendants contended that they would be prejudiced in having to face a stale claim which they were unaware of until five years after the accident and which they had been unable to investigate until six years following its occurrence. The trial judge and the Court of Appeal held that in considering the extent to which the defendants would be prejudiced by the disapplication of the limitation period, compared with the prejudice to the plaintiff, they were entitled to have regard only to the five and a half months' delay since the expiry of the limitation period and not the additional period since the accident. The defendants appealed to the House of Lords.

Held
(1) The appeal was allowed. Section 33(1) gave the court an unfettered discretion to disapply the limitation period, subject only to considering the degree to which the plaintiff and the defendant would be respectively prejudiced. Lord Griffiths said that the court was entitled to take into account the whole period since the accident, including that before the limitation period expired. The balance of prejudice favoured the defendants, who would have a

very difficult task in defending a claim which was based on an occurrence which was now very old, whereas the plaintiff would suffer the relatively minor inconvenience of having to issue proceedings against her solicitors, against whom she had a very strong case for their failure to issue a protective writ when they were first involved.

(2) Lord Griffiths, agreeing with the dissenting judgment of Stuart-Smith LJ in the Court of Appeal, said that although the time of the notification of the plaintiff's claim to the defendant is not one of the matters particularly specified in s. 33(3) which the court may take into account in deciding whether or not to exercise its discretion in the plaintiff's favour under s. 33(1), it is an extremely important consideration. Simply because it is not specifically referred to in s. 33(3) does not mean that it is irrelevant.

Guidera v NEI Projects (India) Ltd
The Independent, 19 February 1990

Court of Appeal (Slade and Mann LJJ and Sir David Croom-Johnson)

Subject matter: Limitation Act 1980, s. 14(1)(b).

In this case the court was called upon to construe the word 'attributable' in s. 14(1)(b) of the Limitation Act 1980.

Held
It meant that there had to be a real possibility, and not merely a fanciful one, that P's injuries were attributable to the act or omission of the defendant. 'Attributable' in the section meant 'capable of being attributed to' and the act or omission in question had to be a possible cause as opposed to a probable cause of the injury.

Stephen v Riverside Health Authority
The Independent, 5 December 1990

Queen's Bench Division (Auld J)

Subject matter: Limitation Act 1980, s. 14(1) — 'date of knowledge'.

P had trained as a radiographer but had not qualified. In 1977, at the age of 44, some 20 years after her own training she underwent a mammography (a breast X-ray). She knew that the radiographer was conducting the mammography in an incompetent fashion. She felt some immediate side effects and developed reddening of the skin, moist spots and other discomfitures. She later learned that she had received a total dose of 34 Roentgen to each breast, instead of the usual eight. However, she was told by several doctors that her symptoms could not have been caused by the radiation exposure unless it was of the order of hundreds or thousands of Roentgen, and that her continuing symptoms were secondary to psychological problems. In 1985 she was told that her symptoms were consistent only with a dosage of radiation which would have increased her risk of developing cancer. A writ issued by previous solicitors was discontinued and in 1988 a new writ was issued. This was nearly three years after the reasonably favourable opinion on her claim. The defendant health authority sought to argue that she had not brought her claim within three years of her 'date of knowledge' under the Limitation Act 1980, s. 14(1).

Held
The plaintiff's suspicions of injury were not sufficient to cause time to begin to run; it was her knowledge which was important. It was not until 1985 that P had the critical piece of knowledge that she had, or could have had, a sufficiently high dose of radiation to cause her symptoms. Her past radiographic experience did not characterise her suspicions as knowledge to set off against the range of highly qualified experts who had reassured her that the exposure levels were not sufficient to cause harm. Auld J held that her claim was not statute barred.

Halford v Brookes
The Times, 28 November 1990

Court of Appeal (Lord Donaldson MR, Nourse and Russell LJJ)

Subject matter: Limitation Act 1980, s. 14 — 'fact ascertainable only with the help of expert knowledge' — s. 33 — court's discretion to override time limit.

CASES

In April 1978 the plaintiff's daughter, aged 16, was strangled and stabbed to death in open countryside near the Trent and Mersey canal in Derbyshire. The second defendant, then aged 15, confessed and was charged with her murder. He later implicated the first defendant, his stepfather. By the end of the trial in November 1978, in which the first defendant denied any complicity, everyone concerned in the case must have been aware, according to Russell LJ, that one or both of the defendants had been responsible for the attack on the girl which had caused her death. The plaintiff's solicitors did not at that time canvass the possibility of civil proceedings, but she and her family continued to press for a prosecution to be brought against the first defendant for murder. It was not until 1985 that the plaintiff consulted new solicitors who raised the possibility of a civil claim in her capacity as administratrix of her deceased daughter's estate. On obtaining legal aid, proceedings were commenced in April 1987. The defendant asserted that they were time barred.

Held

(1) An appeal from the High Court which had discontinued the plaintiff's action as statute barred, was allowed. Where a plaintiff acting as administratrix of her deceased daughter's estate knew (in 1978) that the injuries which had caused her death were intentionally inflicted by the defendants, she had at that date the necessary knowledge to begin proceedings within the three-year time period. Section 14 of the Limitation Act provides that the plaintiff's knowledge is to include that which the plaintiff might reasonably have been expected to acquire from, *inter alia*, appropriate expert advice. But, according to Russell LJ giving the leading judgment, the plaintiff should not be fixed with knowledge of a fact ascertainable only with the help of expert advice, so long as she had taken all reasonable steps to obtain that advice. The plaintiff's submission that she did not have the necessary knowledge until she had received legal advice in respect of her claim, when she acquired the necessary knowledge with the help of legal expert advice could not, however, be sustained. The plaintiff did not require expert advice in order to invest her with the necessary knowledge contemplated by s. 14. She was capable of acquiring that herself, and did so by the conclusion of the second defendant's trial. Where she failed to do so until after the expiry of the period when

she later received legal advice that such facts might found a claim for battery, her claim was *prima facie* statute barred.

(2) However, in exercising its discretion under s. 33 of the Limitation Act 1980, the court was entitled to take into account her ignorance of her legal rights, and that no criticism in respect of the delay could be levelled against her. However, where as here the delay between the expiration of the primary limitation period and the issue of the writ was over six years, that would normally be crucial, since delay could lead to fading recollections and the disappearance of evidence to the extent that a fair trial could not be held. Russell LJ said that that was not fatal in this case. The accuracy of people's recollections was not in issue here; there was no room for mistaken recollection. Taking into account the starkness of the events, the delay was unlikely to render the evidence less cogent. In those circumstances, the court would disapply the limitation period and permit the action to continue.

Bentley v Bristol and Western Health Authority
The Times, 6 December 1990

Queen's Bench Division (Hirst J)

Subject matter: Limitation Act 1980, s. 11.

The plaintiff was injured in the course of a surgical operation. She became aware of this at some later time and issued proceedings, which the defendants sought to have dismissed for having been brought out of time.

Held

For the purposes of the Limitation Act 1980, s. 11 and in respect of personal injury actions involving surgical operations, a plaintiff's date of knowledge that an injury which she had suffered was attributable in whole or in part to an operation did not arise until she became aware of some act or omission which could have affected the safety of the operation. Broad knowledge on the part of the plaintiff that the injury was caused by the operation *per se* was not sufficient to set the limitation period running. The crucial consideration was knowledge of the act or omission which was actually alleged to constitute negligence. In the instant case, that amounted to knowledge of some act or omission which constituted the failure to carry out the operation safely. Where, as here, knowledge of such an act or omission would often depend on information derived by the plaintiff from expert opinion, such opinion could be relevant in determining a plaintiff's date of knowledge.

Jones v *Trollope Colls Cementation Overseas Ltd*
The Times, 26 January 1990

Court of Appeal (Neill and Farquharson LJJ and Sir John Megaw)

Subject matter: Foreign Limitation Periods Act 1984.

This is an important case for overseas travellers which involved consideration of the Foreign Limitation Periods Act 1984. P, a US citizen, was employed by the US Government in Karachi, Pakistan. In May 1984 she met two employees of the first defendants who offered her a lift in their car. One of them drove the car at considerable speed. The car crashed; P was injured and sought to recover compensation from the driver's employers. She was assured that insurers would be in touch with her and waited for them to contact her. Two years passed before she issued a writ in England against the driver and his employers. The question arose of which limitation period applied to the claim; the three year period of the 1980 Act or the one year period allowed by Pakistani law. The Foreign Limitation Periods Act 1984 commenced on 1 October 1985; s. 1(1)(a) of the Act provides that the law of limitation of another country will apply. Section 7(3)(a) exempts actions or proceedings commenced before the appointed day (which clearly did not apply here); and s. 2 provides for exceptions to s. 1(1)(a). Section 2(2) provides for an exception to s. 1(1)(a) where there is a conflict with public policy to the extent that application of the 1984 Act would cause 'undue hardship' to any person who was a party to the action or proceedings.

Held

Farquharson LJ said that 'undue' added something more than just hardship; it meant excessive hardship, or a hardship greater than the circumstances warranted. Here, the plaintiff had been caused undue hardship by her long hospitalisation and the belief that her claim would be met. In the circumstances, this was clearly an appropriate case in which to exempt the operation of the foreign limitation period.

Foster v Turnbull
The Times, 22 May 1990

Court of Appeal (Slade, Russell and Leggatt LJJ)

Subject matter: Service of writs.

The way in which procedural rules can be manipulated and work to produce a case of apparent injustice to apparently deserving plaintiffs is illustrated in this case, which involved the claim by a widow as administratix of her husband's estate against Norwich Union Fire Insurance Society as representatives of the Motor Insurers Bureau. F had been killed in a motor accident involving his car and a motor bike. The driver and pillion passenger of the bike were also killed. It emerged that they had been riding the bike without the permission of the owner and were uninsured, but Norwich Union assured solicitors for the estate that liability was not in issue. A writ was issued against the two deceased riders and the owner of the bike, and Norwich Union asked for service on a named firm of solicitors. After the period for validity of service expired, Norwich changed their solicitors. Those solicitors wrote indicating that orders under RSC Ord. 15 r. 6A (providing for the appointment of a representative of the estate of a deceased who had died before the commencement of proceedings) had not been obtained. The High Court sustained an appeal by the plaintiff against the deputy district registrar's refusal to make an order under Ord. 15 r. 6A and to extend the validity of the writ. Norwich appealed against the High Court's ruling.

Held

(1) Leggatt LJ held that there was no provision, even if an order could properly have been made under Ord. 15 r. 6A(4)(b) (cases where order may be made even though r. 6A(4)(a) not complied with) for that to have retrospective effect because the writ had not been validly served and, in respect of Norwich, had not been served at all, validly or otherwise.

(2) A second question, however, arose. This was that of estoppel. That failed because the estates were no more than

CASES

abstractions; a representation that the first solicitors had authority to accept service on behalf of the estates, even if acted upon, could not help the plaintiff. Service of the writ was not at large; it had to be upon a legal person. None of the available candidates to accept service could have been validly served because they were not a party to the proceedings, and the defendants could not be served because they were dead. An action could not by agreement between solicitors be maintained against non-existent defendants.

Kelly v Dawes
The Times, 27 September 1990

Queen's Bench Division (Potter J)

Subject matter: Structured settlements.

In this case Potter J considered the composition and administration of a structured settlement provision (further discussed in Chapter 4). The case illustrates the way in which the structured settlement can be made to work to the advantage of both plaintiffs and defendants, and underlines the irony of the court approving a settlement which itself it cannot order, as damages awards have still to adhere to the lump sum principle. Presently, the recipient of a lump sum payment is taxed not on the payment but on any income arising from it. That will remain the case where, for example, an annuity is purchased on a person's behalf rather than in their own name. However, the Revenue has agreed with the Association of British Insurers that periodic payments to a plaintiff funded by an annuity purchased by the insurer from a separate life office could be treated as payments of capital rather than income. The effect of this is that the insurer can buy for less than the lump sum which would otherwise have been payable an annuity which would yield higher benefits than the plaintiff could have been expected to derive from a lump sum. The gain to both parties is financed from the resultant tax saving.

Held
(1) Potter J upheld an arrangement in a personal injuries action whereby the parties had agreed that the defendant's insurers invested a proportion of the total sum payable as damages to the plaintiff in an annuity which would provide an index-linked annual

sum for the rest of the plaintiff's life. This resulted in consequential tax advantages to the plaintiff. It was acceptable on this basis for the defendant to reduce the amount which would otherwise have been payable as a lump sum. The judge suggested that the proper approach in cases involving large sums of damages was a two-fold settlement. First, a lump sum payment to cover financial losses down to date of settlement; and secondly, what would amount to a pension payment in respect of future losses. The advantages, which Potter J held to be significant savings in the administration of the fund and guaranteed annual payments on an inflation-proofed basis, clearly outweighed the possible disadvantages, which were a potential lack of financial and investment flexibility once the scheme was established, and a lack of residue for the plaintiff's estate.

(2)   Potter J also set out a blueprint for future applications for approval of structured settlements. He suggested that each application place before the court:

(a)   Counsel's detailed opinion assessing the value of the claim and its constituent elements on a conventional basis; the appropriate lump sum payment or bracket for settlement; and consideration of the plaintiff's life expectancy based on medical opinions.

(b)   An accountant's report as to the fiscal and investment advantages of the proposed structured settlement; with particular regard to the plaintiff's life expectancy and the likely costs of future care.

(c)   A draft of the form of agreement proposed, with confirmation that it fell within Inland Revenue provisions or practice on which the value of the structured settlement depended.

(d)   Where appropriate, confirmation of the approved terms of the agreement by the Court of Protection conditional upon the court's approval of the settlement

(e)   Material which would satisfy the court that there were sufficient funds outside the structured settlement to meet any unforeseen capital needs of the plaintiff, whether by means of the initial lump sum or any other resources available to the plaintiff.

(f)   Material by which the court could be satisfied that the agreement involved secure arrangements by responsible insurers. This might take the form of one of the well-known tariff companies or one of the syndicates operating under the rules and protection of the Lloyd's market.

Chrzanowska v Glaxo Laboratories
The Independent, 13 March 1990

Queen's Bench Division (Steyn J)

Subject matter: Multiplicity of actions.

In the first of two important cases which dealt with the question of multiplicity of actions arising from the same facts, Steyn J observed that the problems of the procedures to be adopted in group litigation should be investigated. It was, he said, desirable that an outline procedure should be prescribed. P claimed damages for an inflammation of the protective membranes of the spine following an injection with a drug called Myodil, manufactured by the defendants. P sought an order that one judge should be appointed to hear all the applications in the trial of the proposed actions, and that any costs incurred should be paid equally between the plaintiffs.

Held

Looking to the procedures adopted and devised in recent group litigation, most notably the Opren litigation before Hirst J, Steyn J held that the order sought in this case was both sensible and just, and under existing rules, one which could competently be made. Assignment of the judge of the Queen's Bench Division to hear group litigation was a matter for the Lord Chief Justice; however, at an early stage of litigation, as here, such an assignment was not necessary. All applications which arose on the Northern Circuit involving the Myodil litigation were to be reserved for hearing by Steyn and Rose JJ. Section 5(1) of the Supreme Court Act 1981 provided that all questions as to costs of and incidental to High Court proceedings should be at the discretion of the court. Here, the order sought would provide as requested for sharing of the plaintiffs' costs, as in *Davies* v *Eli Lilly & Co.* [1987] 1 WLR 1136.

Horrocks v Ford Motor Co. Ltd
The Times, 15 February 1990

Court of Appeal (Lord Donaldson MR, Stuart-Smith and Farquharson LJJ)

Subject matter: Multiplicity of actions.

In this case the Court of Appeal castigated the attempts made by the parties to devise for themselves new procedures to meet the case of large numbers of actions with special features in common. P and a large number of other defendants had issued proceedings against the defendants for industrial deafness, arising in the main out of employment at factories in Essex and Merseyside.

Held
In granting leave to appeal, but dismissing appeals by the plaintiffs against transfer of business from the Brentwood County Court, where the plaintiffs had issued their proceedings, to Liverpool, where most of the actions arose and where most of the lawyers and medical witnesses lived, Lord Donaldson said that it was appropriate for the Court to adopt an investigative approach to see which was the most appropriate forum in which the cases were to be heard. It was not, he said, open to the parties to resort to self help on the basis of what they thought, probably wrongly, were the less busy courts. While standard court procedures were designed for the determination of the general run of claims before the courts, where large numbers of claims with special features in common arose, the courts would devise new procedures specially adapted to such cases. He suggested that, as here, one particular district court could be developed as a specialised court so that cases could be transferred within the jurisdiction to that court. Where it was clear that only a proportion of the cases would come to trial, in these cases about 10 per cent, but it was not clear which those would be, courts could and had refrained from giving dates for trial until a much later stage than usual. However, periods had been earmarked for hearing such cases as came on well in advance. Where, as here, there were few firms of solicitors and few expert witnesses involved, a delay through 'bottlenecking' was more likely to be caused by delays in reaching the point of readiness for hearing than in giving a hearing date. Thus, the courts had taken the initiative in listing cases for

CASES

directions if they appeared to be progressing too slowly. Firms involved in handling such cases as these should give urgent consideration, with the Law Society, to see that they were equipped to take on as many cases as they were being asked to do, and to seek to broaden the base of expert medical opinion on which they could draw.

A series of cases dealing with the questions of interest on damages have occurred in the year under review. The conflicting responses which they have given to one particular question may be conveniently dealt with here.

O'Connor v *Amos Bridgman Abattoirs Ltd*
The Times, 13 April 1990

Queen's Bench Division (Scott Baker J)

Subject matter: Interest on damages.

P claimed damages for personal injury. The remaining question for the court was one of damages, the registrar having granted leave to the plaintiff to enter summary judgment for damages to be assessed. The defendants appealed against this order, arguing that the effect of s. 17 of the Judgments Act 1838 would be to render them liable for an unfairly large amount of interest on damages ultimately awarded. Section 17 provides for interest to be payable on a judgment debt at the current rate of 15 per cent per annum from the date of judgment. This contrasts with the current short term investment rate of 13 per cent, from which the plaintiff would normally expect interest on the special damage at half that rate from the date of accident to judgment; on the damages for pain and suffering at 2 per cent from the date of service of the writ until judgment; and on the future loss, no damages at all. Here, the plaintiff would receive 15 per cent interest on the whole award from judgment.

Held

The fact that the consequences of giving judgment for the plaintiff might result in an unjust result as regards interest on the damages that might ultimately be awarded was not a good reason for depriving the plaintiff of the judgment to which he was otherwise entitled. The court had no discretion under s. 17 as to whether interest on damages and costs should be awarded.

Lindop v *Goodwin Steel Castings Ltd*
The Times, 19 June 1990

Queen's Bench Division (Turner J)

Subject matter: Interest on damages.

In this personal injuries action, liability had been agreed before the court in late 1984 as to 75 per cent of the full damages. Turner J argued that cases such as this raised the 'vexed question' of whether interest ran from the date of the 'liability judgment' or the date of the 'damages judgment'. If interest at the commercial rate ran from the liability judgment then the defendant would be placed under an injustice which produced no countervailing injustice for the plaintiff if it were removed.

Held
Even where judgment as to liability has been entered, interest under s. 17 at the commercial rate was recoverable only after damages had been assessed. In cases where there was a liability judgment and a separate damages judgment, there were in fact two judgments. The judgment debt with which s. 17 of the 1838 Act was concerned was established not in the judgment which fixed the liability, but in that which fixed the amount to be paid. Turner J held that such a construction of s. 17 led to a logical and sensible result and accorded with the plain language of the section.

Wilson v *Graham*
The Times, 25 June 1990

Queen's Bench Division (Drake J)

Subject matter: Interest on damages.

The plaintiff conceded that if judgment debt interest became payable from the date of judgment then interest payable on the damages should cease at that date. In both *O'Connor* and this case the courts followed the House of Lords in *Hunt* v *R M Douglas Roofing* [1990] AC 398, holding that an order for payment of costs was a judgment debt within s. 17 and that interest on costs ran from the date of judgment and not from the later date on which the amount of costs was ascertained on taxation. A similar rule applied in cases where liability preceded the issue of damages.

Comment
In consolidated appeals, this issue was 'leap-frogged' to the House of Lords who gave judgment at the end of the judicial term in mid-December 1990.

Thomas v Bunn
Wilson v Graham
Lea v British Aerospace
The Independent, 14 December 1990; *The Guardian*, 19 December 1990

House of Lords (Lord Keith of Kinkel, Lord Brandon of Oakbrook, Lord Brightman, Lord Templeman and Lord Ackner)

Subject matter: Interest on damages.

In each of these Queen's Bench Division cases, which had arisen either from a road accident or an injury at work, the plaintiff had claimed damages and the defendant had either been held liable or had admitted liability. In each, the judge had ordered interest on the judgment debt under the Judgments Act 1838, s. 17 to run from the date when the damages were ordered to be assessed, rather than the later date (preferred by Turner J in *Lindop*) when damages were actually assessed. The appeals raised several questions as to the special rules as to damages and interest established in recent years. In particular, they called into question the correctness of Lord Ackner's *obiter dictum* in *Hunt* v *R M Douglas (Roofing) Ltd* [1990] AC 398, in which he had suggested that:

> a judgment for costs to be taxed is to be treated in the same way as a judgment for damages to be assessed, where the amount ultimately ascertained is treated as if it was mentioned in the judgment, no further order being required.

Held

The interest payable under s. 17 on an award of damages only begins to run from the later date when damages are finally agreed or assessed and judgment entered for that sum, and not from the earlier date when, liability having been agreed or determined, an order is made for damages to be assessed. It follows from this that the form of judgment suggested by Simon Gottblatt QC (sitting as a deputy judge of the High Court) in *Putty* v *Hopkinson* [1990] 1 All ER 1057, which is either merely declaratory of the liability of the defendant or otherwise in some form which does not attract an immediate charge to interest under the 1838 Act, is unnecessary. Lord Ackner, giving the leading judgment, reviewed the special rules which have recently been fashioned for personal injury cases:

(a) Damages in personal injury actions were assessed not at the date when such damages were first sustained but at the date of trial (*Wright* v *BRB* [1983] AC 773). In most other cases, damages were assessed when the cause of action arose and the successful plaintiff was awarded interest at the commercial rate from that date until judgment (Supreme Court Act 1981, s. 35A; County Courts Act 1984, s. 69). In those such cases the date from which interest on the judgment began to run under s. 17 made little practical difference.

(b) Where death or personal injury was involved, the court was required to award interest in the absence of special reasons for not doing so (Supreme Court Act 1981, s. 35A(2)).

(c) In personal injury cases, the 'conventional award of interest' was awarded on damages for pain and suffering and loss of amenities at the rate of 2 per cent per annum from the date of service of the writ until judgment, and on special damages at half the rate on special investment account from the date of the accident until judgment (*Jefford* v *Gee* [1970] 2 QB 130; *Birkett* v *Hayes* [1982] 1 WLR 816).

Comment

Section 17 of the 1838 Act provides:

> Every judgment debt shall carry interest [at the current statutory rate] from the time of entering up the judgment until the same shall be satisfied, and such interest may be levied under a writ of execution on such judgment.

CASES

Lord Ackner said that if those words were considered in isolation, it was accepted that there could not be a 'judgment debt' until there was a judgment for a quantified sum, that is, a final as compared with an interlocutory judgment. The problem occurred when taking that section in conjunction with s. 18 of the Act. Section 18 provides that:

> All decrees and orders of courts of equity, and all rules of common law . . . whereby any sum of money, or any costs, charges or expenses, shall be payable to any person, shall have the effect of judgments in the superior courts of common law, and the persons to whom any such monies shall be payable, shall be deemed judgment creditors within the meaning of this Act.

A line of cases, down to the House of Lords' decision in *Hunt* v *R M Douglas (Roofing) Ltd* [1990] AC 398, established the principle that interest on awards of costs ran from the date of judgment when the order for costs is made (the *incipitur* rule) and not the later date on which costs were taxed and certified (the *allocatur* rule). Sections 17 and 18 made no distinction between costs and damages, treating each as a judgment debt. Since interest on costs ran from the date judgment was pronounced, logically, interest on damages should do the same, even though in respect of each of the cases under consideration Lord Ackner's own dictum in *Hunt* was not directly applicable because in each of these cases only an interlocutory and not a final judgment had been entered, and hence a further order was required before any sum of money was payable. The plaintiffs contended that it was established in *Hunt* that liability to pay interest on costs did not have to await their quantification, but dated back to the judgment awarding them. That might be anomalous, in that it construed an order for payment of costs to be taxed as a judgment debt within s. 17 even though before taxation there was no sum for which execution could be levied. Accordingly, the plaintiffs argued that the same principles should apply to damages. Section 17 clearly envisaged a single judgment which constituted the 'judgment debt'; Lord Ackner accepted that the *Hunt* rule recognised the anomalous position of an order for costs to be taxed. But, insofar as his dictum in *Hunt* suggested that this extended also to an interim or interlocutory order for damages to be assessed, that was wrong. Section 17 did not relate to an interim order or judgment establishing only the defendant's liability. It related only to a 'damages judgment' which quantified the defendant's liability. In a limited sense of there being an interim or interlocutory judgment and a damages judgment, the House of Lords has adopted Turner J's formulation in *Lindop* that there are two judgments; an interlocutory 'liability' judgment and a final 'damages' judgment. Accordingly, the three appeals were allowed.

With respect to their Lordships, the opposite conclusion seems to be at least as sustainable, if not preferable. Clearly, the policy for which the courts should aim is the speedy conclusion of all proceedings in every case, let alone a personal injuries case. Hence, discouragements to reaching finality on either questions of liability or damages are to be avoided. To give a reason for postponing or delaying the liability issue would be unfortunate; but the same can be said of the damages issue. *Lindop* illustrates this well; it appeared to have taken nearly six years to have arrived at the point where damages could be assessed following admitted or accepted liability. Such a delay verges on the inordinate, and the discipline of knowing that interest will be running from the date of liability would seem to urge a speedier conclusion of the question of quantum. It is clear from the cases reviewed that s. 17 does not have a clear and open meaning, and that judgments as to the desirability of when interest accrues indeed differ. If there does exist a form of pressure which can be applied to the issue of settling or agreeing quantum, then it appears desirable in principle to use it. Whether it would be desirable in some cases to permit for a discretion in the court to decide the date from which interest should run is another matter; that might depend on the behaviour of the parties between the dates of judgment and hearing as to damages. The section does not, however, provide for that and at present the choice is a straight one between liability judgment date and damages assessment date, and the House of Lords has unequivocally chosen the later, damages date.

Gee v *News Group Newspapers Ltd*
The Times, 8 June 1990

Queen's Bench Division (Sheen J)

Subject matter: Interest on costs based on erroneous view as to the law.

This case also concerned the application of *Hunt* v *Douglas*.

Held
In a libel action, an agreement as to interest on costs based on an erroneous view of the law was binding on the parties, as it would be quite inequitable to allow the plaintiff to reopen the matter and argue that interest should be recalculated.

Legal Aid Board v *Russell*
[1990] 3 All ER 18

Court of Appeal (Lord Donaldson MR, Butler-Sloss and Taylor LJJ)

Subject matter: Interest on costs — payment into court.

In this important case the court had to consider an analogous problem which throws further light on these difficult issues. W had been injured in a road accident in September 1984. In due course he claimed damages from the defendant, Russell, and in August 1988 gave notice of his acceptance of monies paid into court amounting to £35,000. The plaintiff, who was legally aided, was concerned to obtain interest on the costs incurred in bringing the claim, since this would reduce the amount over which the Legal Aid Board would have a charge on the damages which W received from the defendant's insurers. Taxation of costs was completed in January 1989; the defendant Russell argued that interest on the amount of costs accrued from that date, whereas the plaintiff W argued that it accrued on acceptance of the monies paid in five months earlier. The costs taxed were £10,200 at 15 per cent interest, such that the sum immediately in issue was only £630. However, the outcome of the case and this appeal is of immense practical significance to the legal aid fund and to motor and other liability insurers. The legally aided plaintiff (replaced by an order of substitution by the Legal Aid Board) was awarded interest on the costs of the action from the date of acceptance of the sum paid into court in settlement of the claim. On appeal, the defendant argued that the streamlined procedure (of RSC Ord. 22 r. 3(4), (5) and (6) and RSC App. A Forms 23 and 24 and RSC Ord. 62 r. 5(1) and (4)), which relieves the plaintiff of any need to apply to the court for an order for taxation of costs where he or she is simply accepting monies paid into court in satisfaction of a claim, has incidentally deprived the plaintiff of any right to interest on those costs. The only case in which this right subsists, it was argued, is where such a plaintiff becomes entitled on the defendant's default of payment within four days of notice of the acceptance of payment in under RSC Ord. 45 r. 15 to sign judgment for the amount of costs outstanding, although even then interest will only accrue from the date of that judgment.

Held
This streamlined procedure avoided the need for the plaintiff to apply to the court for an order on costs and a taxation on costs. The effect of this, incidentally and doubtless accidentally according to Lord Donaldson, deprived the plaintiff of any interest on costs. In *Hunt* v *Douglas* the House of Lords had ruled that the 'time of entering up judgment' within s. 17 was when the order for costs was made (the *incipitur* rule) and not the later date on which the taxation of costs was completed (the *allocatur* rule). Cases such as this involved the acceptance of payment in under Ord. 22 and Forms 23 and 24. The 1838 Act applied only to specific judgments or orders. Acceptance of monies paid in gave rise to an entitlement to costs only under Rules of the Supreme Court, and not under a judgment or order to which s. 17 applied. Although *Hunt* had made it clear that it was not necessary to have a formal judgment or order to attract the operation of the 1838 Act (following *Fisher* v *Dudding* (1841) 9 Dowl 872), it was nonetheless necessary for there to be some record, formal or informal, of a decision that the plaintiff was entitled to costs.

Comment
In *Hunt's* case, the action had not been settled by acceptance of the monies paid in under Ord. 22 r. 3; rather, the parties by agreement came to the court to obtain an order that 'all further proceedings in this action be stayed (except for the purpose of carrying into effect the terms hereof) upon the following terms' which included a term that the money in court be paid out in part satisfaction of the claim, and that the balance be paid within seven days, and that the defendants should pay the costs of the plaintiff. This was accepted by all parties and in the House of Lords to be a judgment or order which carried interest as if it were a judgment within s. 17 of the Judgments Act 1838, and hence that interest on costs was

recoverable. An entitlement arising from the Rules was, according to Lord Donaldson in the instant case, legislative and not judicial in character, and although highly unsatisfactory, was insufficient to allow interest to be awarded under s. 17. The Court argued that the position should be remedied as soon as a new Rule could be laid before Parliament. Alternatively, it must remain open to parties to adopt the formulation approved in *Hunt* and apply to the court for what might be called a *Hunt* order, that the proceedings be discontinued and that costs be payable. Although Lord Donaldson thought that this would constitute a 'wholly unnecessary labour', until Parliamentary time provides an opportunity for this position to be remedied, it appears to be the only sensible course to adopt. It may be thought that if Parliament does take the opportunity to amend s. 18 of the Judgments Act, it might at the same time legislatively sort out the anomalies and difficulties to which *Hunt* and these succeeding cases have given rise.

Doleman v *Deakin*
The Times, 30 January 1990

Court of Appeal (Dillon, Ralph Gibson and Stuart-Smith LJJ)

Subject matter: Administration of Justice Act 1982, s. 3 — bereavement damages.

In March 1984, when the unmarried deceased was 17, he was struck by a car while crossing the road. He sustained severe injuries from which he died nearly six weeks later, just after his 18th birthday. The plaintiffs, suing in their own behalf and as administrators of the estate of their deceased son, sought bereavement damages as provided for in the Fatal Accidents Act 1976 as amended by the Administration of Justice Act 1982. Section 1A provides that bereavement damages are available to parents in respect of the death of a legitimate minor who was never married. The parents appealed against the judge's refusal to award them bereavement damages.

Held
(1) The relevant date for the purposes of the statute in respect of bereavement damages was the date of the death and not the date of the tortious act.

(2) That was so even if the deceased might 'for all practical purposes have been dead after the injury was suffered'. The autopsy evidence, on which the judge was alone entitled to rely, was that the deceased died in April 1984.

Comment
As a footnote, bereavement damages, first introduced and set at a level of £3,500 in the Administration of Justice Act 1982, are to be increased from 1 April 1991 to £7,500.

Schott Kem Ltd v *Bentley*
[1990] 3 All ER 850

Court of Appeal (Neill and Glidewell LJJ)

Subject matter: RSC Ord. 29 — interim payment.

In a case which did not involve a personal injuries claim, but which contains important *obiter* which may change the present approach to interim payments in personal injury cases, the Court of Appeal held as follows.

Held
An award of an interim payment of damages under RSC Ord. 29 does not depend upon the plaintiff showing need for the payment, nor on being able to show that he or she would suffer prejudice if the award was not made. Accordingly:

(1) The customary practice in personal injuries actions for interim payments to be limited to sums for which the plaintiff could show a need was not strictly correct. While it might be a sensible approach to avoid large interim payments in personal injuries cases, because of the difficulties which might arise if an order for repayment were made under RSC Ord. 29 r. 17, there was no implicit restriction in the rules which prevented an order being made in the absence of need or prejudice. Order 29 rr. 11 and 12, which provide that such payments may be ordered by the court 'if it thinks fit', conferred a discretion upon the court whether to order an interim payment at all.

(2) The amount of the payment was expressed to be 'of such amount as [the court] thinks just' with the additional limitation in

the case of damages that the amount was not to exceed 'a reasonable proportion which in the opinion of the court are likely to be recovered by the plaintiff', after taking into account specified matters. There was no further basis for a limitation on the court's jurisdiction to order interim payments.

(3) Addressing himself to the defendants' second submission, that the court should not make joint and several orders for interim payments against a number of defendants, Neill LJ observed that there was no provision for apportionment at this stage of the proceedings, and joint and several orders would enable a plaintiff to select the defendant from whom to recover the interim payment. In the alternative, the defendants had urged that if joint and several orders were made, then the total of those orders should not exceed the amount thought to be 'just' in accordance with Ord. 29 rr. 11 and 12. On this point Neill LJ said that there would seem to be no objection to making orders against two or more defendants in respect of the same liability and in respect of the same sum, if the court was satisfied as to the liability of each of the defendants against whom the order was made. Nor could there be any objection in principle to the making of orders for interim payments against two or more defendants for different fractions of the total amount thought to be just, provided that:

(a) it was made clear that if the aggregate of the fractions awarded against the defendants exceeded the 'just amount', the sum actually recoverable by the plaintiffs could not exceed the 'just amount';

(b) in the case of a claim for damages, it was made clear that the sum actually recoverable by the plaintiff could not exceed the 'reasonable proportion of the damages';

(c) the order was otherwise complied with.

Where, as in the instant case, claims both joint and several were made against a number of different defendants and some where some of the claims were alternative to other claims, the order had to make clear whether the payments ordered against different defendants in respect of the same liability were intended to be for the same sum or in respect of different fractions and, where claims were made against two defendants in the alternative, whether the court was satisfied that the plaintiff would recover against one of the defendants and, if so, which one. It was necessary for the judge to make clear in the order the sums ordered under each head of claim and to indicate whether or not the sum ordered against each individual defendant was intended to be in respect of a separate fraction of the relevant liability. Where, as here, the court had not done that, there was force in the criticism raised by the defendant that the aggregate of the payments ordered exceeded the total liability of which the judge had, at this stage, been satisfied.

4

OFFICIAL PUBLICATONS

Master of the Rolls' Review of the Legal Year 1989-90

Extracts from Lord Donaldson's review of the legal year give some important indications of the way in which practice and procedure in appellate courts will be fashioned in the near future. It contains some extremely timely reminders of the adoption of proper procedural measures and flags some important reforms for which practices should be preparing themselves. Extracts from the review are published in (1990) *New Law Journal*, 9 November 1990, and the most salient points may be noted here:

(a) It is surprisingly often forgotten when seeking to appeal that an application to the court making the order or giving the judgment which is to be appealed should be made seeking an order staying execution.

(b) Order 59 providing that notice of appeal should be served on the other party within four weeks after the judgment to be appealed was sealed, perfected or, in the county court, given that it does not in itself, validly give notice of the appeal. Such service of itself has no value unless the appeal is also set down with the Court of Appeal itself. Wholly avoidable expense and wastes of time are incurred with applications for extension of time for appeal when the Civil Appeals Office informs prospective appellants on enquiry that they know nothing of the proposed appeal. Such applications are in future likely to be refused unless the proposed appeal appears to have sufficient merit. Indemnity fund beware!

(c) The Courts and Legal Services Act 1990 gives the Rule Committee power to undertake a fundamental overhaul of the complex and illogical categories of appeal in which it is necessary to seek leave (presently set out in 1991 Supreme Court Practice at note 59/1/25). The Rule Committee intends to exercise this power in a thoroughgoing fashion.

Practice Note
Transfer of damages awarded in the Queen's Bench Division to the Court of Protection
(1990) 42 *Law Society Gazette* 35

Where a plaintiff who is a patient within the meaning of the Mental Health Act 1983 is awarded damages in a Queen's Bench Division action, the transfer of those damages to the Court of Protection will be facilitated if the judgment includes a provision to the following effect:

> . . . that the defendant do within X days pay the said sum of X into court to be placed to and accumulated in a special account pending an application by the next friend to the Court of Protection for the appointment of a receiver from the plaintiff and that upon such appointment being made the said sum of X together with any interest thereon [subject to a first charge under the Legal Aid Act 1988] be transferred to the Court of Protection to the credit of the plaintiff to be dealt with as the Court of Protection in its discretion shall think fit.

Any order which approves a compromise of an action brought by such a person should include a similar provision. Once an award has been made, there are several steps which can be taken to expedite matters in such a case. These should be taken by solicitors involved in the action.

First, an application should be made on a form available from the Public Trust Office, Stewart House, 24 Kingsway, London WC2B 6JX for the appointment of a receiver in anticipation of the damages to be awarded. The application is usually made by the next friend, who may also be the most suitable person to act as receiver. Secondly, where the plaintiff was legally aided, the statutory charge will operate so as to freeze the account. A reserve for costs should be agreed with the Legal Aid Board on appropriate forms available and then negotiable through local area offices. An order should then be obtained from the court making the award directing the court funds office to release to the area office the amount from the award to cover the statutory charge. The balance will be released to the Court of Protection when the Part II order has been lodged. This is an order made following the preparation of a payment schedule (Form 200, 6th Cumulative Supplement to the Supreme Court Practice 1988).

Practice Direction
Supreme Court Taxing Office
[1990] 2 All ER 512

A new list of counsels' interlocutory fees for accident cases was issued by the Chief Master, F. G. Berkeley, on 15 May 1990. They came into operation in respect of instructions or briefs delivered on or after 1 March 1990. Except in the case of conference fees, the fee is intended to cover any necessary perusal of papers in connection with the item. A lower fee may be appropriate where the item has not been dealt with comprehensively, was unusually simple, or where more than one item has been dealt with simultaneously. If a higher fee has been agreed upon, it will need to be justified upon taxation, as will any fee which is claimed whether included in the list or not.

	Personal injury cases (excluding road traffic accidents)	Road traffic accident cases
Statement of claim	£55	£40
Defence without counterclaim	£50	£35
Defence (plain admission)	£15	£15
Particulars—request	£24	£24
answers	£30	£30
Reply with or without defence to counterclaim	£30	£30
Third party notice (not to stand as statement of claim)	£30	£30
Interrogatories and answers	£50	£50
Advice on evidence	£60	£60
Opinion (including opinion on appeal)	£40	£40
Opinion on liability	£50	£50
Opinion on quantum	£50	£50
Opinion on liability and quantum	£80	£80
Opinion on liability, quantum and evidence	£130	£130
Notice of appeal to Court of Appeal and counternotice	£50	£50
Brief on summons before master	£40	£40

Conference fees
Queen's Counsel £60 for first half hour, £30 for each succeeding half hour
Junior counsel £35 for first half hour, £20 for each succeeding half hour

Practice Direction
Queen's Bench Division
[1990] 1 All ER 800

Ian Warren, the Senior Master of the Queen's Bench Division issued the following direction on 5 February 1990:

> As from 1 April 1990 the County Court Rules will no longer require a certificate of judgment to be signed by the registrar (see CCR Ord. 22 r. 8(3), as inserted by the County Court (Amendment No. 4) Rules 1989, SI 1989 No. 2436, r. 23). Such a certificate will, as from that date, be required to be signed by an officer of the county court concerned. The Practice Direction which was issued on 14 November 1988 ([1989] 1 WLR 403; [1988] 3 All ER 1084) is accordingly amended in relation to certificates bearing date after 1 April 1990 by substituting the following for para. 2:
>
>> 2. The judgment counter clerk will check that the certificate has been signed by an officer of the issuing court (a rubber stamp is not sufficient) and dated and that the certificate complies with CCR Ord. 22 r. 8(1), and in particular with the requirement that on its face it states that it is granted 'for the purpose of enforcing the judgment [or order] in the High Court.

Crown Indemnity Scheme
Department of Health Circular (HC(89)34)

The circular (HC(89)34) is issued to regional, special and district health authorities and outlines the arrangements for dealing with claims of negligence. From 1 January 1990 a new scheme for the indemnification of NHS medical and dental staff sued for negligence was introduced. The new scheme gives health authorities and not defence unions responsibility for the payments of awards and settlements against medical and dental staff employed in the hospital and community health services. The indemnity scheme will not affect the options open to injured patients or their advisers, but it may be that it will make the settlement of claims more speedy. Internally, it will have more impact, for although internal administrative arrangements are left at the discretion of individual authorities, it will have the effect of making the precise attribution of causal responsibility for an injury more important. For example, if a hospital authority can point to a delay in the admission of a patient by a GP, or even unreasonable delay by the patient themselves, a way of off-loading some of the damages to be paid may be available. The department's circular makes it clear that in negotiating settlements of claims health authorities are to have regard to possible conflicts of interest between the health authority and any such outside general or dental practitioner, and that consultation with the intention of deciding how the claim should be processed, should be entered into. Where necessary or appropriate, negotiations should be fostered which will apportion the damages payable and the associated costs, and this should be done preferably before action. The circular also enjoins health authorities to pay attention to the views of any practitioner involved, and any potential damage to his or her professional reputation, a matter which is to be taken into account when making decisions about settlement. Similarly, the circular states that 'clear regard' is to be paid to 'any point of principle or of wider application' to which the case gives rise, as well as to the costs of the case.

EC Council Directive 90/269/EEC (OJ L 21 June 1990, p. 9)

Two important EC Directives on health and safety have been issued in 1990. In Council Directive 90/269/EEC (OJ L 21 June 1990, p. 9) the Council has laid down minimum health and safety requirements for handling of loads where there is a risk in particular of injury which must be implemented by national legislation by the end of 1992. This clearly has important consequences for those involved in advising employers and union solicitors who will want to monitor the implementation of the directive's requirements. The application of the directive is not expressly excluded from any area of work, and is without prejudice to the wider requirements of Dir. 89/391/EEC. The 'manual handling of loads' is defined by the 1990 Directive as any transporting or supporting of a load, by one or more workers, including lifting, putting down, pushing, pulling, carrying or moving of a load which (by reason of its characteristics or of unfavourable ergonomic conditions) involves a risk particularly of back injury to workers. Article 3(1) requires employers to take appropriate organisational measures or use appropriate means to avoid the need for the manual handling of loads by workers. Where this is unavoidable, appropriate measures or means must be taken to reduce the risk involved, having regard to the characteristics of the load, physical effort required, characteristics of the working environment and requirements of the activity ('reference factors', art. 3(2)). A further obligation is placed on employers by art. 4 to organise work stations so as to make handling of loads as safe and healthy as possible, and to assess the health and safety conditions of the type of work involved, to examine the characteristics of loads and to exercise care to avoid or reduce the risk by taking appropriate measures, with regard to the characteristics of the working environment and the requirements of the activity; again account must be taken of the 'reference factors'.

Articles impose a duty on employers to provide information on the measures taken to implement the provisions of the directive; to give, where possible, precise information as to the weight of loads, the centre of gravity of the heaviest side where a load is uneven; and to provide training and information on how to handle loads correctly and on the potential risks, having regard to the 'reference factors' and individual risk factors, such as an individual's physical suitability for the task, the suitability of working clothing, and requisite knowledge and training.

EC Council Directive 90/270/EEC (OJ L 156 21 June 1990, p. 14)

Minimum health and safety requirements which must be met, again by the end of 1992, for work with display screen equipment have also been published (Council Directive 90/270/EEC, OJ L 156 21 June 1990, p. 14). Workers are to be entitled to an appropriate eye test before commencing work on a display screen, at regular intervals thereafter and whenever visual difficulties mean that the work might affect them (art. 9(1)). 'Display screen equipment' is defined in the directive to mean an alpha-numeric or graphic display screen, regardless of the display process employed. There is a definition of 'worker' for the purposes of the directive, which makes reference back to the definition of worker in Directive 89/391/EEC; as any worker within the scope of that directive who habitually uses display screen equipment as a significant part of his or her normal work. This directive does not apply, however, to drivers' cabs or control cabs for vehicles or machinery; computer systems either on board a means of transport or mainly intended for public use; portable systems not in prolonged use at a workstation; calculators, cash registers or any equipment having a small data or measurement display required for direct use of the equipment, or typewriters with a window (art. 1(3)). Employers are required to make an evaluation of any threats to safety and health posed by display screen equipment, particularly any posed to eyesight, physical problems or mental stress, and to take such remedial measures as are appropriate (art. 3). Article 4 prescribes minimum standards for workstations opened after the end of 1992; those opened before that date must be upgraded where necessary by 1996. In a far reaching provision, art. 7, it is provided that a user's work schedule must be planned to ensure that work at the display screen is periodically interrupted by breaks or changes of activity. The importance of these preventative measures is profound; they are attempts to address two major aspects of workplace personal injury which cause massive financial losses to industry on a recurrent basis. Although each will initially be costly to implement, the investment in safety and health which they represent should be repaid over the long haul.

Provision of Service to the Inner London Residuary Body: Personal Injury Claims (ILEA)

Pursuant to the Education Reform Act 1988, ss. 176(1) and 183(1), the Secretary of State for Education made directions dated 30 March 1990 providing that personal injury actions against the Inner London Education Authority (which ceased to exist on 1 April 1990 by virtue of s. 162 of the 1988 Act) should be dealt with by the London Residuary Body. All claims in respect of personal injury sustained prior to 1 April 1990 by former employees of ILEA or members of the public, students, or other visitors to property of ILEA are to be dealt with in this way. Similarly, the Secretary of

State has directed that LRB shall satisfy out of its own resources any such claims for which it may be found liable, together with the legal costs and other expenses. Where the Inner London Education Authority appears in the title of an action as defendant to any such claim, the name of the LRB may be substituted without an order giving leave to amend or carry on the proceedings.

5

COMMERCIAL PUBLICATIONS AND OTHER IMPORTANT SOURCES

Butterworths Personal Injury Litigation Service
Iain Goldrein and Margaret de Haas, Butterworths,
2 vols., £145.00

An indispensable publication for all practices whose caseload involves a heavy personal injuries bias. The contents cover personal injuries; fatal accident practice and procedure; motor insurance and third party rights; practice and procedure; costs; legal aid; a series of valuable appendices and pleadings, advice on quantum and a series of quantum judgments. The loose leaf service is updated regularly.

Kemp and Kemp: The Quantum of Damages
David A. Mcl. Kemp, Sweet & Maxwell, 2 vols., £220.00
(1990 service £110.00)

For practitioners who need to keep up to date with quantum issues there is no alternative to Kemp & Kemp. The two volumes deal quickly and comprehensively with recent additions to the enormous wealth of quantum judgments and precedents. Volume I covers the law and practice applicable to personal injury; the same applicable to Fatal Accident Act claims; classified awards under the 1976 Act; and appendices which contain copies of the major statutory provisions and specimen pleadings in FAA claims, and full pecuniary compensation notes. Volume II concerns injuries of utmost severity such as quadriplegia, paraplegia, very severe brain damage and such like. It deals furthermore with multiple injuries; head and skin injuries and those to the senses, spine, internal organs, and other bodily parts.

Articles on Structured Settlements

The use of structured settlements in large personal injuries actions has become increasingly common since they became a realistic possibility in July 1987 following the agreement negotiated then between the Inland Revenue and the Association of British Insurers. Their use has now been considered, approved and guidelines laid out for their administration and operation in *Kelly* v *Dawes, The Times*, 27 September 1990, considered above. The value of these and the way in which they are put together was examined by Dennis Hulls of Structured Compensation Ltd in (1990) *Law Society's Gazette*, 21 March 1990, p. 27 (and see Henry Witcomb 'Structured Settlements — an Unexploited Opportunity' (1990) *New Law Journal*, 26 January 1990, p. 88). A structured compensation award is composed of two elements: the less familiar concern of lawyers, in the interests of both plaintiffs and defendants, to begin comprehensive personal and vocational rehabilitation as soon as possible after the accident, which is often delayed because of the present structure of the compensation system; and, more readily identified, a system which seeks to improve upon the delivery of benefits, whether providing for medical requirements or additionally for the income and capital requirements of the victim, which the lump sum award poorly delivers.

One of the major deficiencies of the lump sum award is that it delivers to victims, most of whom will have been wage earners, a capital sum about which they receive little advice. A recent study demonstrated that 50 per cent of accident victims have nothing of their lump sum left after one year; that 70 per cent had dissipated it after two years, and that within three years of award 90 per cent of injured plaintiffs who successfully recovered damages had nothing of their award left for their future care and security. The temptation to delay all but the most rudimentary rehabilitation until after the settlement or trial is a major cost of this system, and it postpones or even negates possibilities for recovery of some semblance of pre-accident normality. Hulls advocates the replacement of the lump sum payment system with one which would include periodic cash payments for specific expenditure linked to a timely programme of co-ordinated rehabilitation. In each case, both elements of the package should be individually tailored.

For awards under £50,000 an annuity or structured settlement may not be cost-effective, taking into account the costs of management expenses during the lifetime of the plaintiff and the tax implications. Some form of financial planning, although not necessarily an annuity, is important for sums up to £250,000, but for major awards over this figure an annuity structure is imperative. Basically, a structured settlement would provide for future loss of earnings with periodic payments. More sophisticated packages would be individually tailored to include the provision of an index linked income, payment of health care, provision of increments for the replacement of medical appliances, education and support for dependants. Other items could be factored in as required. Such payments would normally be funded by an annuity purchased by the defendant's insurance company. Tax implications can be planned for with careful use of an appropriate form of scheme. Capital Gains Tax, from which the traditional lump sum is exempt, and income tax liability can be reduced by adopting one of the schemes approved by the Inland Revenue. The Revenue envisage four basic forms of annuity which would qualify for the resulting payments to be treated as capital and not income, which has major advantages for both plaintiff and defendant. The forms are basic terms (where the plaintiff wants the periodic payments to run for a pre-set period and consists of a series of pre-set amounts); index terms (same, except that the periodic payments are inflation-proofed by having them rise in accordance with the retail price index); terms for life (for cases where the periodic payments, in set amounts, continue until the date of the plaintiff's death, with the option to have the agreement subject to a pre-set minimum number of payments) and indexed terms for life. A large sum settlement, such as might apply in a medical negligence case for example, with damages of around £750,000 could be structured in such a way as to increase the plaintiff's annual receipt of periodic damages compared with interest on a lump sum basis by around £5,000 per year and produce a capital saving for the defendant of nearly £40,000. As Hulls demonstrates, this has major advantages for plaintiffs and defendants.